From Alms to Liberation

FROM

ALMS

TO

LIBERATION

The Catholic Church,
the Theologians, Poverty,
and Politics

Werner Levi

PRAEGER

New York
Westport, Connecticut
London

Library of Congress Cataloging-in-Publication Data

Levi, Werner, 1912-
   From alms to liberation : the Catholic Church, the theologians,
poverty, and politics / Werner Levi.
     p. cm.
   Bibliography: p.
   Includes index.
   ISBN 0-275-93171-4 (alk. paper)
   1. Church work with the poor—Catholic Church. 2. Liberation
theology. 3. Catholic Church—Doctrines. I. Title.
BV639.P6L48 1989
261.8'325—dc19   88-29009

Library of Congress Catalog Card Number: 88-29009
ISBN: 0-275-93171-4

First published in 1989

Praeger Publishers, One Madison Avenue, New York, NY 10010
A division of Greenwood Press, Inc.

Printed in the United States of America

The paper used in this book complies with the Permanent
Paper Standard issued by the National Information Standards
Organization (Z39.48-1984).

10 9 8 7 6 5 4 3 2 1

Copyright Acknowledgments

The author and publisher are grateful for permission to reprint from the following sources.

Ricardo Planas, *Liberation Theology: The Political Expression of Religion* (Kansas City,
MO: Sheed & Ward, 1986), p. 61.

John Eagleson and Philip Scharper, eds., *Puebla and Beyond* (Maryknoll, NY: Orbis Books,
1979), pp. 60, 128.

Excerpts from *Economic Justice for All: Catholic Social Teaching and the U.S. Economy,*
Copyright © 1986 by the United States Catholic Conference, Washington, D.C., are used
with permission.

Reprinted with permission of Macmillan Publishing Company from *Pope, Council, and
World: The Story of Vatican II* by Robert B. Kaiser. Copyright © 1963 by Robert Blair
Kaiser.

The Papal Encyclicals, 1740-1981, ed. by Claudia Carlen, I.H.M. (Wilmington, NC:
McGrath Publishing Company, 1981), v. 3, p. 146.

Contents

PART I
The Church, the Theologians, and Poverty

The Pastoral Constitution on the Church in the Modern World, *Gaudium et spes,* 1965 no. 4, one of the documents emerging from the Second Vatican Council, proclaims "Today, the human race is involved in a new stage of history. Profound and rapid changes are spreading by degrees around the whole world. . . . Hence we can already speak of a true cultural and social transformation, one which has repercussions on man's religious life as well."

Prominent among the contemporary changes is the universal demand for the abolition of poverty, injustice, and inequality among men and nations. The novelty lies in the intense and urgent character of the demand, not in the existence of the evils. Poverty and injustice have been afflictions of human society for thousands of years. They have been religious subjects since before Christ preached the Sermon on the Mount. Saints, priests, nuns, religious, and laypersons have devoted, and sometimes sacrificed, their lives to help the poor. The Roman Catholic church (hereafter the church) has claimed historically to be the church of the poor.

For nearly two thousand years churches have had a quasi-monopoly in the Western world on dealing with poverty. Yet, leaving aside the question of the degree of failure or success, poverty still exists as a most serious scourge in the world. At the same time, over the last two hundred years, the Roman Catholic church, like other churches, has gradually lost its quasi-monopoly. In dealing with poverty and the poor, it was forced to compete with the ideologies and activities of secular institutions, especially governments, and sometimes the poor themselves. It had to abandon its traditional, relaxed approach, consisting mainly in pacifying the poor with alms in this world and the promise of a better life in the next. It took a long time to do so.

The church had difficulty in making the transition. Foremost among the unrecognized underlying reasons were, first, that the industrial revolution changed the character of poverty. It was quantitatively different. As industrialization increased, so did the poor. It was qualitatively different. Poverty was accompanied by a higher degree and worse kind of human oppression and exploitation (slavery or near slavery apart!), and the difficulty of escaping it was greater. The personal relationship between employer and employee was replaced by the cash nexus. Finally, the issue of poverty became more secularized than ever before. The second reason was the inadequacy of the theological underpinning which hitherto justified the church's handling of poverty also to serve the new poverty. This new poverty undermined the traditional theology. The two did not match. The subversive character of the new poverty became all the more evident as the secular competitors of the church, in analyzing the causes of poverty and suggesting cures, demonstrated implicitly and sometimes explicitly the insufficiency of the church's approach.

Making the transition required recognition of the novel character of poverty, which the church delayed. Once recognized, an adjustment in traditional theology would become necessary. Doctrinal adjustments had, in principle, often been made by the church, but usually cautiously and always slowly. Moreover, the ecclesiastic and secular political consequences were important considerations in any doctrinal innovations, and, in the case of poverty, they could be risky.

For almost one hundred years after the industrial revolution became socially effective on the European continent (around the beginning of the nineteenth century), the official church rejected changes. This conservative attitude was perhaps the main reason why, in all the trials and tribulations the church endured during this period politically, the complex of poverty played virtually no part. Giving alms and promising a better life in the Kingdom of Heaven could hardly antagonize governments, and pleased the ruling classes, the church's allies.

Moreover, and paradoxically, under the influence and pressure of the church, its traditional philanthropy was largely taken over by the state. Civil legislation and mass political resistance preempted religious activity. If the church wanted to remain the leader and relevant in this field, it would have to be flexible and adaptive. For a long time it was not. Hence the complaint of Pius XI that the loss of the working masses to the church was the greatest scandal of the nineteenth century.

This quiescent situation underwent change around the turn of the twentieth century. The pressures from the political and social conditions in Europe, the danger to the Catholic church of becoming irrelevant, the urging of theologians and elements within the clergy for innovation were among the causes producing the "social encyclicals" beginning with *Rerum novarum*, 1891, and continuing ever since. The old rhetoric was not adequate anymore. The change from feudalism to capitalism with all its early and rather sudden misery for the workers was clearly generated by some men, with other men rebelling against it. There was no credibility in blaming Divine Providence. No longer could the church make God responsible for poverty. Poverty was not inevitable. It was a human creation. Initially, the consequences were not foreseen. The new teaching seemed essentially a change in rhetoric and theology, politically harmless. The secular political powers voiced little objection. But a step nearer to the political arena had been taken.

Then, during the 1960s, Vatican II and Liberation Theology arrived. Their twin emphasis was upon liberating people from material evil as well as spiritual evil on religious grounds. A weighty social, economic, and political—a "worldly"—dimension was thereby added to religion. The clarification of this additive required social analysis for which Marxism offered one obvious instrument. The consequence was the confirmation of findings by pre-Marx theologians, that poverty derived from evil people and their social structures. Its amelioration required their change, and social change meant political action. Liberation turned into a politically explosive issue. The explosion was defused because the idea of the welfare state had already been widely accepted. Nevertheless, to the discomfort of the official church, the poverty issue was now fully in the political arena.

Its politicization was enhanced because changing sinful structures was acknowledging the possibility of collective sin. Purification from sin was no longer an individual's private affair. Donating to charity was insufficient. Those benefitting from these structures considered their change a threat to vested interests. Individually, they could do nothing about it. Collectively, they welcomed a loosening of the bonds which had hitherto tied church and oligarchies together. The result has been that dealing with poverty by the church, and the role Liberation Theology was to play in it, has created much controversy over ecclesiastic and secular politics. This controversy provided the subject for this book.

That Liberation Theology, under that name, had most of its protagonists in Latin America (and coopted the Ecclesiastic Base Communities there, as well), can be substantiated by all the conditions in that subcontinent. Contemporary Latin America is therefore also an area excellently qualified for an examination of politics as they are practiced within and by the church, states, and private groups in relation to a social issue and its wider implications. This is all the more the case as the situation regarding poverty in mid- and late-twentieth century Latin America replicates in many respects conditions of the early industrial revolution in Europe.

The similarities can serve as a touchstone for the church's behavior toward social affairs. Do the social encyclicals prove merely the flexibility of ecclesiastic rhetoric or a willingness to guide and support action? True, the church has no troops, no parliamentary representatives. But she has Liberation theologians and Ecclesiastic Base Communities, each in their way eager to generate the changes so strongly advocated nowadays in the encyclicals.

At the same time, such an examination will also clarify the role of theologians in the politics of the church. Then and now their concern was to keep religion relevant when contemporary conditions were rapidly changing. The nineteenth century theologians were predominantly dealing with the sociological aspects of the social problem of poverty. The Liberation theologians are, in addition, attempting to reinforce the temporal aspects of their solution of the poverty problem with a new interpretation of an underlying theology. They have attempted to systematize and reinterpret Catholic doctrine—with the help of social science—to keep it abreast of today's "profound and rapid changes." They are hoping thereby to stimulate action and give direction to what have been vague dissatisfactions and scattered goals of improving the living conditions of the poor in conformity with Catholic teaching.

This broadening of the foundation for dealing with poverty should not disguise the fact that some of the essence of the theology, foremost the sociological part, did not emerge ready-made from the minds of the contemporary theologians. Much of the thinking, analysis, and agitation of early nineteenth century theologians and of some clerics broke new ground. And in view of the role that Marxism plays in the present-day controversy over Liberation Theology, it should be pointed out that many of the ideas condemned today as Marxist were expressed by theologians and clerics in the nineteenth century before Marx was born. Unfortunately for the persuasiveness of the Liberation theologians' social analysis, Marxist categories remained a major factor. In the context of contemporary Latin American–United States relations, economic and financial analysis beyond mainly social analysis is also a significant element with explanatory power in the Latin American and other Third World situations. But it lacks the appeal and sweep of Marxist analysis. Yet it can be ignored only at the cost of exhaustiveness and accuracy in the explanation of the Latin American situation (which will be the focus in this book).

1
The Church and Poverty: The Nineteenth Century

Almost one hundred years passed before the official church acknowl-edged the new character of poverty in Europe. Preoccupation of many groups inside and outside the church with the "Social Question," as the poverty problem was then called, did not affect the church's practices or its Magisterium. On the contrary, in justification of its traditional practice, popes published numerous encyclicals confirming and theolog-ically reinforcing it. This conservatism of the church was not surprising. It is an inherent feature for many reasons and can explain much of the dif-ficulty bedevilling relations between church and Liberation theologians.

The church is a continuing institution. It is the trustee of a doctrine of divine origin, not static but also not easily accommodated to changing historical conditions beyond nebulously defined limits. For, the church teaches, no part of doctrine is ever discarded or nullified. Such a drastic measure cannot happen since word and tradition are of holy origin. The inviolability of doctrine extends to the Magisterium because the authentic interpretation of God's word is undertaken in the name of Christ. Changes or even reversals in fact taking place are explained not as sub-stitutive but cumulative. They are not even presented as changes but as an accommodation, interpretation, or further development of doctrine, enhancing the understanding of God's word, acknowledging what had always been there but was unrecognized.

A more mundane reason for the church's conservatism was its guard-ianship, at the beginning of the nineteenth century, of an historic legacy making it and the papacy into a worldly power as much as an evangelizing institution. It was associated with, or was itself a secular force still at a time when that force was doomed. It was trying to safeguard its survival by its own means, or, failing that possibility, by associating with the powers that be, basically regardless of their nature. It therefore developed a mentality intolerant of new forces considered dangerous to its existence and regardless of their popularity or strength. This mentality caused it to remain allied in the nineteenth century to the *ancien régime* long after its intellectual and substantive demise. It had thus acquired the character of a reactionary organization, and mostly acted like one, when the modern age dawned on the world. It forfeited its potential impact on shaping that age. Many decades were to expire before the official church could reconcile itself to being a moral more than a political power. During Vatican II Pope John XXIII drew attention to this change when he said "The Church has always opposed . . . errors, and often condemned them with utmost severity. Today, however, Christ's bride prefers the balm of mercy to the arm of severity. She believes that the present needs are best served by explaining more fully the support of her doctrines, rather than by publishing condemnations."[1]

Individuals, whether clergy, theologians, or laypersons, can more readily afford to be progressive. They have always been free "from the worldly fetters" that trammeled the church in past ages (Pope John XXIII). They are not hampered by 2000 years of tradition from applying new knowledge and inspired creativity to an analysis of poverty's causes and cures.

Another factor, also more political than theological, making the church more conservative than other parties, is the unequal status in politics and, it follows, unequal inhibitions in assuming clear-cut positions. The official church in Rome is more exposed than local churches, local churches more than individuals. Whenever there is controversy, its outcome will affect the church politically more than the other two parties. Controversy can touch upon the distribution of power within the church; upon relations between the central church and states or local churches and local governments; upon the international status of the church. Naturally, the church wants to have a decisive influence upon the outcome of controversies in order to control their consequences.

Its instruments are the centralized power in Rome, its hierarchical structure, and ecclesiastic sanctions. Their employment is often only marginally related to theological points because theology can also have political impact. This possibility has affected the debate on the Social Question in the nineteenth century and affects the debate on Liberation Theology in the twentieth.

Yet another factor besetting the official church but hardly the other two parties is their constituencies. Those of the theologians and the local churches are relatively small and relatively homogeneous. The constituency of the central church is global and composed of groups with a multitude of different experiences, values, standards, and political conditions. Caution and even ambiguity become imperative under these circumstances.

The church has tried to cope with that problem by announcing that specific solutions for general problems may have to be adapted to different localities and circumstances. Of necessity, any solution must be sufficiently indefinite to fit various situations. Innovations must be incremental not radical. In his social letter, 1971, Pope Paul VI said in *Octogesima adveniens* nos. 1-4,[2] "In view of the varied situations in the world, it is difficult to give one teaching to cover them all or to offer a solution which has universal value. This is not our intention or even our mission." And as matters in the world became ever more complex, Pope John Paul II said ten years later, in *Laborem exercens* no. 1, "It is not for the Church to analyze scientifically the consequences that these changes may have on human society."

Yet that escape from the dilemma is unhelpful when the very definition of the problem varies from constituency to constituency, as it could in the case of poverty. A poverty level in the United States is a luxury level in many a Third World country, indeed, may not even be recognized as a problem there. Neither the urgency, magnitude, nor means for solving the problem in one country may even be approximately applicable to another country. The specific complications this difference produces in discussions of poverty and social inequalities between the Liberation theologians and the Vatican will be seen later on. But they are an illustration of the theological and secular effects the difference in constituencies can have on the attitudes of the official church and the theologians.

The conservatism of the church was responsible for the incongruous practice of continuing to deal with twentieth century poverty in the manner it had used for hundreds of years. This remained true even after it had, theoretically, acknowledged a different quality in poverty between that of the eighteenth and twentieth centuries.

Customarily the official church was alleviating poverty through charity, translated practically into alms giving. The Christian duty of charity was considered fulfilled by the one-way manner of giving by those who have to those who have not. Little spirit of brotherhood and much paternalism were evident. Neither equality nor justice was given much thought. Changing the status of the poor was not pondered by the official church. The reasonableness of this "solution" of the poverty problem was based on the premise that poverty resulted from the inequality of people, and was, at any rate, a divinely ordained fate in a society created by God. Had not Matthew (26.11) said, "ye have the poor always with you"? Numerous encyclicals (e.g. *Nostis et nobiscum,* 1849; *Quod apostolici,* 1878) used or misused this theme to declare poverty a possible blessing.

Three causes of poverty were emphasized by the church during the nineteenth century, virtually all referring to individuals rather than social conditions. While the contemporary church rarely refers to these causes today, it has not totally discarded them. Occasional references to them reflect the power of traditional thinking and the influence of similar secular arguments voiced by defenders of capitalism.

The first cause was poverty and inequality as the work of God. Those affected by these evils were consoled with the promise of reward in heaven for their suffering on earth. *Nostis et nobiscum,* 1849 no. 22, comforted the poor "that they should not be sad at their condition, since their very poverty makes lighter their journey to salvation, provided that they bear their need with patience and are poor not alone in possessions, but in spirit too." *Quod apostolici,* 1878 no. 9, like many other encyclicals, asserted that social inequalities following from natural inequalities among humans, were established "by Nature." The faithful poor passed on this "truth" from generation to generation, with occasional rebellions against it by the doubters.

The second cause, often repeated and stressed, was seen in the avariciousness of the rich and their sinful accumulation of an overabundance of worldly goods at the expense of the poor and through their exploitation. Pius IX and almost every one of his successors castigated that "unbridled and damnable self-love and self-interest that drive many to seek their own advantage and profit with clearly no regard for their neighbor. We mean that thoroughly unsatiable passion for power and possession that overrides all rules of justice and honesty and never ceases by every means possible to amass and greedily heap up wealth" (*Quanto conficiamur moerore,* 1863, no. 10).

A third cause of poverty or inequality was discovered in the laziness or unjustifiable ambition of workers. They were themselves made responsible for their misery. This normally favorite capitalist argument appeared in church documents only toward the end of the nineteenth century and was carried unadulterated into the twentieth. In *Laetitiae sanctae,* 1893 no. 5, Pope Leo XIII criticized the distaste for "a simple life" evinced in the tendency of a worker "to shrink from toil, to become discontent with his lot, to fix his gaze on things that are above him, and to look forward with unthinking hopefulness to some future equalization of property." In *Longinqua,* 1895 no. 17, he reminded people that "God has ordered that different classes exist in the human race."

With remarkable stubbornness, the church adhered to this line of argumentation, even while toward the end of the nineteenth century it very slowly inaugurated another parallel line more reflective of a growing awareness that a new society would need adaptations in its traditional teaching and political stance.

Pope Leo XIII still claimed in 1902 that "nature" required different classes to remain where they were. His successor, Pius X assumed the same position and warned in *Iucunda sane,* 1904 no. 22, Catholic writers not to emphasize such causes of poverty as might provoke an aversion among the poor against the rich. We must "live contented with the state in which Providence has placed us, while striving to better it by the fulfillment of our duties, to thirst after the future life in the hope of eternal reward." He also reminded young priests that dedication to studies in various branches of learning was useful; dedication "to the welfare of souls" was preferable.

In 1914 Pope Benedict XV in *Ad beatissimi apostolorum* no. 12, asserted "the position of each one is that which each by use of his natural gifts—unless prevented by force of circumstances—is able to make for himself." The striving of the poor against the rich was "contrary to justice and charity," as well as "irrational," the more so as the poor "by honest industry can improve their fortunes if they choose." As late as 1959, Pope John XXIII in *Ad Petri cathedram* no. 42, amplified by declaring that all classes are readily accessible to everyone. "Anyone who is diligent and capable has the opportunity to rise to higher levels of society." (In November, 1986, the Lay Commission on Catholic Social Teaching and the U.S. Economy blamed the poor's lack of moral grounding for poverty.)[3]

These papal views were not just stated as a matter of routine from time to time. They were part of a campaign of criticism and condemnation of "liberal" (i.e. democratic) and socialist thoughts expressed by religious and secular individuals and groups during the long, great debate on the nineteenth century Social Question. They represented the carefully considered position of the official church on the problems of the working class following the arrival and development of the industrial revolution on the European continent. They were also meant to be the official answer to the many theologians, clerics, and religious laypersons whose concern was an adjustment of Catholic church doctrine and practice to the new social conditions created by the industrial revolution.

By treating poverty and inequality as inevitable appurtenances of society as ordained by God, a conservative and tradition-minded church obviated the need to become actively involved in the process leading to fundamental improvements. This exegesis served the church and conservative oligarchies with which it was usually in collusion as opposing change in a system benefiting both parties, in the distribution of goods both possessed, and in the aloof and paternalistic relationship prevailing between the church and the poor masses of the faithful. The question was not raised whether the Christian vision of a person's fate in a future world could be realized without freedom from crushing poverty and a recognition of human dignity in this world. In dealing with poverty, the church excluded an analysis of its social roots. It limited itself to cosmetic improvements in the form of narrowly conceived charity. No thought was given to basic social changes.

This attitude was as true of nineteenth century Europe as it had been until recently in Latin America. It was responsible for the impression large sections of the population had formed of the church: that it had joined with anti-historical forces and become a defender of the status quo. Pope John XXIII presumably had this situation in mind when he stated at the opening of Vatican II Council that the church had failed to keep up to date with the changing conditions of this modern world, and when he appealed to the Council to open up the church to the modern world.

2
The Theologians and Poverty: The Nineteenth Century

Throughout the nineteenth century, numerous Social and Liberal Catholics recognized the novelty of the social situation created by the industrial revolution. They were aware that the oppression of the workers was creating an explosive situation requiring remedies to which the Catholic church could make a substantial contribution. The editors of the *Ere Nouvelle* wrote in the middle of the nineteenth century, "We do not believe these evils to be without remedy; and if patience is enjoined for everybody, charity combined with science can accomplish something to stay the scourge, if not destroy it entirely."[1]

Some Catholics bemoaned the "indifference" shown by Catholics toward the Social Question. Others called for the creation of a school of Social Catholicism to develop a social science for saving Catholicism, lest a secular social science might destroy it. Many argued, in a substantial deviation from the teaching of the church, that not only individual evil people, but the entire social system they constructed were responsible for the fate of the industrial workers. They were aware, as was the church, of the political risks that tampering with the social system would bring. Both accepted them. The difference between the two was mainly that, as it turned out, the theologians chose to ride the wave of the future, while the church was trying to stem the tide.

The reaction of these individuals to the political, industrial, and intellectual revolutions of the nineteenth century showed, in comparison with the church, a more open mind, fewer inhibitions, and a greater willingness to reinterpret or accommodate Catholic doctrine. They also saw the misery and some of them actually lived with the workers (not dissimilar to some Liberation theologians living today in the Ecclesiastic Base Communities).

They felt less threatened than the church by the intellectual currents and movements. They did not, as did the church (e.g. in the "Syllabus of Errors," 1864), evaluate the innovations in their extremes and worst possible light the more easily and justifiably to reject them. Instead of fighting innovations, they sought to reconcile them with Catholicism. They discovered early that the poverty of the industrial workers had different roots from the poverty of the preindustrial age. They distinguished decades before the church did, or admitted, industrially caused poverty from pauperism. They discovered in the industrial workers a new class, for whose integration into the existing society appropriate mechanisms were lacking and had to be invented. These individuals did not share the church's optimism that the members of the working class could work themselves into a higher class or that the rich would balance class disadvantages by augmented charity. They expected the decreasing religiosity of modern societies to be permanent. The religious values still affecting the institutions of feudal life (e.g. the responsibility of the master for the apprentice) would be replaced by the laws of "pure economics," that is, value-free economic laws, with morality functioning in a separate section of human activity. Nor did they share the church's confidence in the occurrence and effectiveness of conversion to overcome the evils the industrial revolution generated. Altogether, they believed strongly in the man-made nature of the new evils and, hence, the possibility of man to undo them.

As the Social Question arose in France[2] earlier than in other parts of the Continent, theologians, laymen, and clerics became active there earlier than those in other countries. At the same time, relations between church and state, interaction between political and social factors, and factionalism among Catholics were much more complex in France than anywhere else. Yet, there was no precedent to guide the thoughts and actions of these people, resulting in a great diversity of analyses and proposals.

Although a great number of different labels were attached to these various individuals, they shared a common ground. They all searched for an alleviation of the industrial workers' distress. They all realized the novelty of the situation, and especially the system-caused, not divine, nature of poverty.

Several of these individuals had a following, and common concerns eventually created contacts with Catholics in other European countries, but no effective movement ever developed. This fact had two disadvantages. These Catholics could not compete successfully with fast-growing secular movements, foremost socialism; and the church could counteract them with considerable efficiency. In the short run, the church looked upon these Catholics with hostility for theological or political reasons, or both. In many instances the church was successful in suppressing their ideas or activities, not unlike what is happening to some Liberation theologians in Latin America today. In the long run and by the time many ideas of these Catholics had generally been accepted also outside the church, it finally adopted them. In the meantime, however, the delay cost the church a heavy price in adherents and influence for which, especially in France, it is still paying today.

Pierre S. Ballanche, for instance, warned in 1818 that the "plebs" would not tolerate their lowly position much longer and would revolt against the rich as the responsible party. M. de Bonald, though a monarchist, criticized the single-minded quest for wealth and the new industry which was unable to feed the children it produced. Many others at this early time related the un-Christian pursuit of wealth to the arrival of the machine, which they also condemned as an instrument for the exploitation and oppression of the workers. Philippe Buchez, a Christian and a revolutionary (who, however, rejected class war as un-Christian) referred in 1829 (when Marx was 11 years old) to the division of the industrial society into two classes, one owning the means of production, the other having to sell itself to the first class to eke out a living, with the inequality between the two continuously enlarging. He indicted the system in the name of Christian principles and of the Christian church, whose only mistake was not to be revolutionary!

Contemporaries and successors of these men were less radical politically, but equally inspired by the prevailing poverty in developing their analyses. Félicité Lammenais and J.-B.-H. Lacordaire were prominent among them. Frédéric Ozanam, originator of the term *Christian democracy,* published a document at age 18, in 1831, calling for acting out, not merely preaching Christian principles. He blamed the class struggle as the moving force for the unfortunate history of his time. Catholics should be mediators between rich and poor. He insisted long before the church did that the function of Christianity was to make people happy on earth as well as in heaven (Liberation Theology!). This would require restraints upon economic liberalism (i.e. capitalism), especially the free market for workers and goods, considered by him the main cause of the dehumanization of workers and their degradation into a commodity.

Avariciousness was considered the cause of poverty by these men as well as the official church. But the church stopped there for many decades. It was thus relieved of the need to analyze the new social system. It was enabled to remain allied to the ruling class. It could also criticize these men and even punish them for contravening the church's teaching and supporting the "wrong" side in the controversy, to boot.

For these men, affirming the avariciousness of the rich was merely the starting point in their search for improvements. They understood that the basic problem was not merely the existence of some rich people behaving sinfully but their having erected a social structure that gave free rein to their behavior.

As the revolution of 1848 approached, they were hoping to exploit its social more than its political aspects. But they failed. They received no support from the official church. On the contrary, some of these men were severely condemned occasionally and the writings of a few were placed on the Index.

Following the revolution, progressive Catholicism suffered a setback in France, or even death. It suffered from the chasm between the official church and an alienated proletariat, as well as the church's negative answers to the Social Question, robbing it of relevance to the conditions of the time. An anti-clericalism developed, surviving unto this day. Luckily for the continuation of progressive Catholicism, as the idea was quieting in France, it obtained growing prominence in Germany.

The German progressive Catholics were, in general, less radical than their French colleagues.[3] They could afford to be, as the position of the Catholic church in Germany was much easier than in France (in spite of the Kulturkampf, 1871-1882). The settlement of church-state relations lacked the depth, extremism, and virulence of that in France. The problem of the German Catholics was less the form of the state than the acceptance of Catholic ideas within the accepted form. State intervention was less resented because the state showed more sympathy toward the Catholic church and Catholics. Last but not least, advances in social legislation toward the end of the century made the Catholic progressives appear less radical. Withal, however, their influence upon the official church was only slightly greater than that of their French colleagues. Comparable situations prevailed in the Netherlands, Belgium, and Austria.

Many Catholic thinkers in these countries addressed themselves mainly to the possible reconciliation between Catholicism and secular intellectual currents or to the political role of Catholicism (as e.g. Georg Hermes, the German professor of theology whose last two books were condemned by a papal bull in 1835). Others, many popes included, reverted back nostalgically to the corporate, paternalistic state of the Middle Ages (which did not necessarily save them from their writings being Indexed, as e.g. Joseph von Görres, a publisher of newspapers, journals, and books, who in his late years, 1836-1842, wrote about Catholic mysticism).

Outstanding among those dealing directly with the Social Question was Franz von Baader. He published his early writings in 1834 and 1835, when Marx was 16 years old. He insisted that Christian feelings must be translated into social reforms through action. He blamed the "argyrocracy" (moneyed class) for the workers' distress because they were using their power selfishly and in an antisocial, un-Christian manner. Making the workers poor was to him a form of paganism. In his study of 1835 he pointed out the new qualitative character of poverty produced by the industrial revolution. The debased "poor and powerless" had only their labor to sell and were at the mercy of the "powerful and propertied." He remarked that he had written his essay "The Proletariat, Its Plight and Misery"[4] to draw attention to the problem of "finding the proletariat its rightful place in the community." Granting "individual liberty" unrestrained by social considerations would simply return the people to "slavery," making them either "land serfs" in the country or "money serfs" in industry.

The best known, not the most imaginative, but probably the most influential theologian after von Baader was Wilhelm von Ketteler, bishop of Mainz. His backward-looking remedies for poverty indicated that he was fundamentally a conservative person. But he strongly condemned "liberalism." He described capitalism as dehumanizing and an insult to God. The church's duty, he argued, was to rescue workers, not just spiritually but materially as well. Though he was critical of "liberalism" and socialism, he counseled that whatever was good and useful in each should be adopted. His influence reached all over Europe and eventually affected the first "social" encyclical *Rerum novarum,* 1891.

A great number of individuals and groups all over Europe could be found who shared these and similar views. Their appeals to make the church more relevant to the plight of the workers went unheeded in Rome until almost the end of the century. These men found little understanding in the Vatican. They also failed to obtain a substantial following. Their relative failure at that time may have been due in part to their inability to join together and create an impressive comprehensive theory that could have made an impact, not merely on fellow theologians or the clergy, but also the mass of the faithful. It might also have impressed non-Catholic circles and allowed social Catholicism to compete more successfully with secular ideologies. Instead, almost everywhere on the Continent, socialism and, for different reasons, Protestantism gained much headway over Catholicism. Neither the Catholic church, nor the progressive theologians possessed the psychological appeal of Marxism. Neither had the credibility with the masses that socialism enjoyed. Neither showed the determination to break with the status quo, or, in the case of the church, even the *ancien régime,* that socialism demonstrated and the masses of the workers wanted. Neither was proposing the itinerary to a better world here and now that Marxism submitted to a receptive population.

3

The Foundation of the Church's Attitude in the Nineteenth Century

---

Throughout most of the nineteenth century the official church assumed a rigid, uncompromising position. It was aggressively negative toward social and intellectual developments. It refused to consider dispassionately the views and proposals of the more forward looking clerics and theologians. It tried to come to terms with political and social innovations by forcing them into the outmoded framework of its interpretations and methods. If they did not fit, they were rejected. The roots of this behavior were the determination to maintain tradition at all cost, an ingrained reluctance to touch doctrine and Magisterium, and a misjudgment of the political circumstances of the times.

The church developed its stance largely as a defense against the growth of intellectual and political movements that threatened, and indeed in some cases interfered with, the integral survival of the church and its power. The Vatican had decided that radical opposition to innovations of almost any kind and maintenance of the status quo by almost any means would best safeguard the existence of the church. Deviations from this policy occasionally occurred, but usually only in the absence of an alternative and mostly too late to prevent some loss of power and status.

The position of the church was hardened by its perspective that in the debates raging around the Social Question, it considered itself to be the main target of attack when, in fact, the Social Question itself was the focus. The result was, as René Coste has pointed out, "the all too frequent deficiency of Christian communities and theologians in the analysis of historical reality. Taken altogether, the churches of the nineteenth century Europe were not aware of the extent of the change in society resulting from industrialization. . . ."[1]

Identifying the nature of this change and developing appropriate solutions for the ensuing problems would have required an investigation of its roots. Such an enterprise by the church was not possible for two reasons. First, analyzing and then theorizing about the character of society was not considered a church mission. Second, the change was rejected a priori because it was held responsible for the difficulties of the church.

Pope John XXIII, in opening Vatican II, 1962, alluded critically to that position of the church when he described it as believing that a rotten world was rejecting the church, when it should have been that progressing, social change required the church to make itself relevant.

Until almost *Rerum novarum,* 1891, the encyclicals expressed the most traditional viewpoints and condemned the new intellectual and political movements sometimes in the most vitriolic language. Poverty and the poor were discussed as they had been for hundreds of years, according to the most conservative interpretation of revelation and tradition. The avariciousness of the rich was forever condemned, coupled with appeals for more charity. Once in a while, attempts were made to specify vaguely a dividing line between a reasonable and an unreasonable accumulation of wealth, but never with sufficient specificity to trouble the conscience of the rich. Another approach would have been difficult in any case. The differences of wealth in different parts of the church's constituency were too great. And the church never determined how much poverty was due to Divine Providence and how much to human greed.

This difficulty could have been diminished, had the church made use of the newly discovered difference between modern-type poverty casued by industrialization and old-type pauperism. Instead, however, this distinction was noted only to be rejected. The inevitable consequence was inadequacy of the cures for poverty suggested by the church.

There are a number of reasons the combined effect of which could explain the position of the church.

The assumption of poverty and inequality as appurtenances of a human society created by God permitted, almost demanded, that humans not do anything fundamental about it. The effect of this approach to poverty, as modern theologians—and by now the church itself—point out, was surely not intended by the founders of Christianity. It rested on a failure to distinguish between the religious and secular meaning of poverty (in addition to ignoring the difference between industrially caused poverty and pauperism). Purely material poverty imposed from without is the Marxist-type poverty, usually narrowed to the proletariat at that; the poverty not praised but actually condemned by the Gospel.

The evangelical poverty deserving blessing requires an element of voluntarism. It is, as Karl Rahner[2] and later Gustavo Gutiérrez have written, an "attitude of the heart," having little to do with the lack of earthly values. Or as Roger Haight pointed out, "Probably the most basic fundamental experience underlying liberation theology is the *experience of poverty.*"[3] "*Poverty*" here means lack of the essential necessities of life. "*Experience*" is not limited to those materially poor, but includes those aware of the situation, outraged by it; and who condemn it, feel guilty about it, and have a sense of responsibility about it. Poverty in spirit is thus shared by a circle reaching beyond the materially poor. It becomes a social phenomenon and can serve for what later became known as social sin. Consequently alms giving does not satisfy the Gospel's demand for charity. Charity requires brotherhood and love, identification with the poor, and suffering with them. A community. The Chilean bishops in 1973 decried mere philanthropy and humanitarianism as fulfillment of the Gospel's demand for charity.

The secular interpretation of charity as alms giving was politically useful to the church. By appealing to individual donors, by making alms giving a matter of conversion, the alleviation of poverty was placed on a personal, discrete level. The social system was not affected, the political system remained untouched, the politicians could proceed undisturbed, the church was saved from having to deal with politics and could continue to cooperate with the powers that be. These were at least the expedient effects, if not the motivations, of the church's dealing with poverty in its customary manner.

Insisting on this interpretation in the face of challenges to it even from within the walls of the church also satisfied the church teaching that doctrine cannot be revoked, corrected, replaced, and so on. A new viewpoint would have to be introduced in the form of interpretation, accommodation, and expansion of doctrine. The minor initial adjustment was made, eventually and reluctantly, that, since people were responsible for poverty, thereby corrupting God's work, they must be sinful people. Causing poverty was then ascribed to sinful behavior, not yet social structure. Conversion of the sinner would thus be the means of abolishing poverty and inequality; there was no need for the church to engage in social analysis—an odious enterprise anyway.

The church's negative attitude was also justified by the dualism between spirit and matter. This view was hundreds of years old and had been elaborated in innumerable philosophies. Matter (materialism) was something corrupt, disturbing preoccupation with ideas and the higher things in life. It was a necessary evil, almost a tool of the devil. As having to deal with material things hampered a person's spiritual growth, there was an inclination among Christians to look down upon activities and things of this world. Remains of this mentality are still noticeable today in the official church's unending censure of Liberation theologians for placing spiritual and material welfare on the same level, and in its hesitancy to acknowledge the concept of total liberation.

There were further, less theological, reasons for the church's delayed adjustments to modern conditions. The church's centuries-old near-monopoly of dealing with poverty and the poor in the Western world was coming to an end. With the industrial revolution came philosophies, theories, analyses, proposals, strategies, institutions, and activities to undo its side effects. The church's monopoly position was challenged from many sides. The poor obtained an option between the church and secular ideologies and institutions for taking care of their misery. In the competition with secular appeals referring to very visible causes of the workers' fate and promising improvements here and now (e.g. socialism) the church very often lost out, mainly because of its inability or unwill-ingness to adjust its teachings. Actually, its choice was limited. The church could not very well adopt many of its competitors' ideas without betraying some of its fundamental teachings, at least it could not do so within the necessary time span to retain all its following. And the enormous pluralism in its worldwide constituency prevented it from changing its teachings in regard to one group and not the others. On the contrary, it placed a premium upon trying to stay out of these worldly matters in an endeavor to remain on good terms with all believers and their governments, which was in any case the church's inclination to do.

Furthermore, there was no great pressure from the mass of the church's followers to change its stance. The influential public of the church was involved in the Social Question mostly to the extent only that its own welfare was directly affected. The majority of the faithful came from the countryside anyway, unaware of the urban workers' plight. The higher ranks of the ecclesiastic hierarchy were recruited from the upper classes. Catholics, like their church, interested in politics, economics, and social affairs were preoccupied mainly with the potential dangers threatening them from novel ideologies and unaccustomed social ac-tions. They rarely suspected a link between these innovations and the fate of the urban proletariat. Their concern focused more on the rela-tions between church and state than on the living standards of the indus-trial workers.

There was, finally, the general political climate of the nineteenth century driving the church into its conservative position. The official church had greater worries than the Social Question, or so it seemed to it, embattled at various times on many fronts, feeling the Faith and perhaps its very existence threatened. The political revolutions and upheavals of the century, the industrial revolution, the non- or anti-religious intellectual currents were interpreted in Rome as a conspiracy against the church's spiritual and temporal leadership, and often correctly so. Many experiences of the popes proved traumatic. They chose to fight developments rather than join them, if doing so had been possible at all. The initial reaction of the popes was understandably defensive as well as antagonistic to risky-appearing innovations. They placed themselves thereby, willy-nilly, on the side of like-minded secular groups—eventually the capitalists and, in Latin America, the land-owners. Yet, these were the groups against which many popular, political, and intellectual movements were directed and eventually became victorious in large parts of the Western world.

The nineteenth century church thus emerged as one of those groups often supporting the absolutist and reactionary system of the Restoration, and, in any case, opposing the demands for liberty in all spheres of society and frustrating the growing nationalism. On both these grounds the power of Rome was questioned and, of course, Rome could not very well make them its own. There is a remarkable parallel again between this situation and Latin American Liberation Theology. One of its attractions is a nationalist opposition to the Europeanization of the clergy or, in its more extreme form, a nationalist opposition to what is considered to be an imperialist front composed of a reactionary church, neo-colonialist multinational corporations, and imperialist governments allied to local governments.

After the turn of the nineteenth century, the official church at last added sinful structures to sinful men as causes of poverty. This new emphasis renewed the search for cures by the church and eventually theologians. The mid-twentieth century theologians found it more necessary than their predecessors to have the church adopt their findings into the official teaching and activities, mainly because of the greater influence of secular social sciences on their thinking. This proved a difficult—though not entirely unsuccessful—undertaking for mainly two reasons.

One reason was that secular social thought had advanced rapidly, had made an impressive impact on Western society, but was unacceptable to the church in many respects. The church therefore had to find its own interpretation of modern social developments, differing sufficiently from secular interpretations to remain true to its fundamental doctrine and identity. The related other was that the growth of socialism, collectivism, totalitarianism, and, eventually, the Third World to prominence generated problems thought to be quite different from preceding ones, yet requiring solutions urgently. Though this was largely a question of politics, namely determining the position of the church in these bewildering and uncertain developments, it was also realized that, in fact, these problems too often arose in part as a result of poverty, inequalities, and social injustice. A continuation or return to preoccupation with the causes and cures of poverty was therefore called for in order to find solutions inspired by doctrine and Magisterium. The official church responded to the call. The development of Catholic social thought became one of the characteristics of the twentieth century church, and, by the middle of the century, once again of the theologians as well, generating what became known as Liberation Theology.

4
Causes of Poverty: The Church View in the Twentieth Century

In a Lenten message, 1877, the bishop of Perugia approvingly quoted Montesquieu's statement that the church should ensure human felicity on earth as well as in a future life. When the bishop became Pope Leo XIII, his encyclical *Rerum novarum*, 1891, initiated at last the church's gradual admission that the causes of poverty might not be altogether God's work. It enabled Pope John Paul II, in *Laborem exercens*, 1981 no. 2, to claim that the "social question" had been the issue for almost one hundred years (in other words one hundred years after the Social Question arose) toward which the church's teaching had been especially directed.

Rerum novarum was hailed as a watershed in the church's concern with social problems. So it was indeed, compared to the church's own past stand. It was conservative when compared to the social thinking and experimenting by secular and Catholic individuals and groups, even some governments' social legislation, preceding the publication of the encyclical. The encyclical itself acknowledged that it was following rather than leading in dealing with the Social Question. The pope had been affected, positively and negatively, by the torrential intellectual currents of the time: progressive Catholic, Marxist, liberal, democratic, rational, materialist, and others. It could not have been easy for him to digest them for integration into the doctrine, although he did not have to start from a clean table. The early church, for example, had opposed usury or a debtor pledging his personal freedom as unacceptable causes of poverty. Sir Thomas More had described a causal relationship between private property and sin—including poverty and inequality.

In general, the church and canon lawyers had discussed the relationship between the rich and the poor in society, what the responsibility and the obligations of the one to the other should be, and how the status and use of property should be regulated. By the time the encyclical appeared, there was no novelty in pinpointing the cause of poverty in the works of humans and their social system. New was only that the idea in such comprehensiveness appeared in an encyclical, and, most important, it signaled the beginning of change in the church's teaching.

Already before the publication of *Rerum novarum,* 1891, the terminology of some encyclicals began to coincide increasingly with that used by the progressive Catholics and even Marxists. Key words like *class, exploitation, oppression,* and *proletarization* had appeared with greater frequency. After publication of the encyclical, criticism of the behavior of the rich heavily outweighed that of the poor. They were asked to use their wealth for the common good. Limitations upon the free use of private property were more insistently emphasized, combined with positive prescriptions of how a good Christian should use wealth. From thereon, a line of argumentation was inaugurated (with only rare relapses, e.g. in *Divini redemptoris,* 1937), gradually leading in the second part of the twentieth century to a severe critique of capitalism and socialism—although some reference to the "natural condition" of poverty was never quite abandoned by the church.

The process of adjustment was careful and slow. Several decades elapsed before the church expressly and fully accepted the widely recognized fact of structural, systemic causes of poverty, though the debate about their specific nature never ended. The qualitative difference between some causes of poverty in the capitalist system and the causes of pauperism were at last acknowledged. *Quadragesimo anno,* 1931 nos. 60, 61, stated that the status of the nonowning worker "is to be carefully distinguished from pauperism." Society must strive to make certain "that at least in the future the abundant fruits of production will accrue equitably to those who are rich and will be distributed in ample sufficiency among the workers. . . ." After suggesting a number of ways of achieving this end," the pope asserted "two things are especially necessary: reform of institutions and correction of morals" (no. 77). This view had inevitable consequences: Christian charity was no longer an adequate solution of the modern poverty problem and Christians must now attempt to produce changes in the nature of modern societies.

Quadragesimo anno, 1931, introduced a new spirit into the church's concern with poverty. Once the belief was established that poverty could be produced by people, the necessity arose to discover what in the behavior of people and in their social system caused some individuals to be rich and others poor. A chain of encyclicals began, supplemented by corresponding statements from bishops' conferences in many countries, accusing the free market and competition, the misuse of the tools of production, national and international capitalism in general, and many kinds of other institutions and social structures of modern societies as contributing their share to poverty and great inequalities. The accusation started cautiously and discreetly, with language clothed in moral terms. Toward the end of the twentieth century it was specific, outspoken and often formulated more in the terminology of social science than religion.

In 1939, for instance, *Summi pontificatus,* no. 59, in stressing the importance of subordinating material success to higher moral values, called the state's "noble prerogative and function" to "control, aid and direct the private and individual activities of national life that they converge harmoniously towards the common good." *Evangelii praecones,* 1951 no. 17, warned of the danger of "the prevalence of atheistic materialism." *Haurietis aquas,* 1956 no. 174, regretted the decline of charity in favor of "the false tenets of *materialism* being propagated in practice and theory, and unbridled freedom of lust everywhere extolled. . . ."

Mater et magistra, 1961 nos. 74, 75, 83, 97, 113, reminded the faithful that the economic order which weakens the workers' dignity, sense of responsibility, or freedom of action, is unjust. It insisted workers must have the right to participate on all levels of the state's economy; and the right to private property should be spread "through all ranks of the citizenry." In *Pacem in terris,* 1963 no. 22, attention was drawn to the right of property as not including its use to impoverish others and "it is opportune to point out that there is a social duty essentially inherent in the right to private property." (Pope John Paul II was to speak of a "social mortgage" on private property later.)

Subsequent papal statements became ever more pronounced. *Gaudium et spes,* 1965 nos. 66, 67, 69, 71, proved almost revolutionary. To wit: "If the demands of justice and equity are not satisfied, vigorous efforts must be made . . . to remove as quickly as possible the immense inequalities which now exist." "It too often happens . . . that in one way or another workers are made slaves of their work. This situation can by no means be justified by so-called economic laws." "[A] man should regard his lawful possessions not merely as his own but also as a common property in the sense that they should accrue to the benefit not only of himself but of others." "If a person is in extreme necessity, he has the right to take from the riches of others what he himself needs." Where "gigantic" rural estates lie idle "for the sake of profit" while the majority of the people are without land, "there is evident and urgent need to increase land productivity." Frequently landless peasants receive wages "unworthy of human beings" or are "exploited" by middlemen. They "live under such personal servitude" that any "fulfilment of their individuality or sharing in the life of the community is ruled out." "Reforms must be instituted" to improve the livelihood of these peasants and "insufficiently cultivated estates should be distributed to those who can make these lands fruitful."

Populorum progressio, 1967 nos. 24, 26, once again castigated the selfish use of private property, this time especially of land, which, when it is "extensive, unused or poorly used" or brings hardships to people, fails to serve the common good and causes social detriment. While, next, the blessings of industrialization are counted, the encyclical also said, "it is unfortunate that on these new conditions a system has been constructed which considers profit as the key motive for economic progress, competition as the supreme law of economics and private ownership of the means of production as an absolute right that has no limits and carries no corresponding social obligation. This unchecked liberalism leads to dictatorship rightly denounced by Pius XI as producing 'the international imperialism of money.' One cannot condemn such abuses too strongly by solemnly recalling once again that the economy is at the service of man." This type of capitalism has been the "source of excessive suffering, injustices and fratricidal conflicts whose effects still persist."

Pope John Paul II, in *Redemptor hominis,* 1979 no. 16, and even more in *Laborem exercens,* 1981, and *Sollicitudo rei socialis,* 1988, summarized comprehensively the evils of modern societies and their resulting misery for people in the developed and developing countries. Like encyclicals before his, he placed the blame on consumerism and unethical attitudes. But he was more outspoken than the others by questioning the social legitimacy of "the financial, monetary, production and commercial mechanisms that . . . support the world economy." These mechanisms cannot remedy the "unjust social situations inherited from the past," or deal with "the urgent challenges and ethical demands of the present." There must be an "effective search for appropriate institutions and mechanisms," through the "indispensable transformation of the structures of economic life" in a Christian spirit. He added that abolishing poverty and inequalities had in this century assumed a world dimension necessitating the transformation of unjust structures on a universal level to which the masses have no access.

These quotations are, of course, taken out of context in the sense that the religious considerations by which they are surrounded in these encyclicals are left out. But, especially when the popes' remarks about total liberation comprising worldly and heavenly happiness are remembered, it may be said that the religious pronouncements do not qualify the social analysis but are its source. They also affect, as will be seen, the cures proposed to deal with the evils of capitalism as the popes have described them. It is indeed the appearance of the social analysis in the context of its religious foundation which gives the late social encyclicals their unique character.

5

The Liberation Theologians and the Causes of Poverty

The beginning of Liberation Theology at its time and place was not fortuitous.

The early 1960s were a period of questioning the nature of existing societies everywhere, especially in respect to cleavages between rich and poor, social justice, political participation of the masses, and the marginalization of entire sections of populations. Much lip service, at least, was paid to an ever-widening scope of humanitarianism. In many parts of the world, debates were followed by action, sometimes peaceful, sometimes rebellious, and often oppressive. In many places, the official church was in a quandary. Issues of its primary concern became politicized. Remaining outside the debate was impossible. Joining it forced the church to abandon its preferred position of steering clear of politics, or perhaps more truly, of not admitting openly its political position.

The trend toward humanitarianism found a favorable echo among many Latin Americans, where political, economic, and cultural conditions were lagging far behind in most states. The time seemed proper to take advantage of the worldwide concern. The Liberation theologians seized the opportunity.

For centuries the official church could not or did not want to overcome the results of its participation in the colonization of Latin America. The close cooperation between the cross and the sword in the conquest of Latin America had consequences still effective today, concretely or psychologically. During the decade of the 1960s sections of the church in parts of Latin America loosened the bonds tying it to the secular oligarchies. But its activities to implement a "preference for the poor" left much to be desired in the minds of many Latin Americans. So did mild attempts of the church to become truly universal instead of being, in reality, a Europeanized church. As originally in Europe, so in Latin America, the church was and some sections still are inclined to side with the powers that be. These were and are in most of Latin America the commercial, landholding, and military classes, with neither particularly concerned about the poor masses either in the urban centers or in the agricultural areas. The early occasional behavioral deviations of the lower clergy or missionaries devoting, even sacrificing themselves to the welfare of the poor, could bring no significant improvements to the misery of the peasant masses and, later, the urban proletariat.

Among the thoughtful individuals turning into analysts and interpreters of prevailing social conditions in the mid-twentieth century could be found the Liberation theologians. By the time Liberation Theology developed, a number of points had been agreed among all parties— popes, some high and low clergymen, theologians—at least in principle. Liberation could not be limited to the traditional religious concept but had to include material liberation. Poverty was both the result of sinful behavior by people and social structures. Classes composed and often divided societies and were here to stay. Violence was to be used, if at all, only in the most exceptional cases. The poor would have the preferential interest of the church.

What was left, mainly, for the Liberation theologians to do was to reinforce these points; elaborate upon them; give them a thorough, modern theological foundation; apply the Gospel in the Latin American context; or, amounting to the same thing, give the Catholic church a distinct Latin American identity and, above all, initiate and provide guidance for the translation of these ideas into action.

They were helped in fulfilling their task by the climate of the times, which also affected the church to some extent.

The Second Vatican Council (1962-1965) had an enormous liberalizing effect. In particular, it decisively abandoned the church's negative stance toward the world and its modern development. On the contrary, it provided guidelines on how the church, with its continuing emphasis on otherworldliness could and must reconcile its major mission with the conditions of this world. As Ricardo Planas sums up the result of Vatican II, especially in regard to its effect upon the development of Liberation Theology, "The Council, indeed, paved the way for a spiritual renewal, one in which the antagonism between heaven and earth, spirit and matter, and the love of God and the love of the person diminished considerably. The Church and Christians have begun to orient themselves toward 'the duty to build a better world based upon truth and justice,' while acknowledging that temporal activity does not hinder one's spiritual growth in Christ."[1]

The social encyclicals of the middle twentieth century and those after Vatican II greatly added to the impact of Vatican II upon the modernization of the church. Their criticism of orthodox capitalism, their assertion of the primacy of the peoples' needs over capitalist principles, their demand for a more equitable distribution of wealth, their imposition of limits upon the use of private property, their condemnation of the exploitation of landless peasants and industrial workers were closely related to the search for the causes of poverty. They all seemed tailor-made to apply to Latin American conditions. They clearly affected the frame of mind in which Liberation Theology was developed, and served to stimulate and support it.

There were many Latin American conferences from which, sometimes rightly, sometimes wrongly, the Liberation theologians took comfort and support for their findings of the causes of poverty. Political and social events in parts of Latin America (especially the rise of Fidel Castro in Cuba and the fate of the Brazilian revolution of 1964) further raised questions in people's mind about the nature of their societies never broached by the traditional church. Latin America was in ferment.

In 1955 the first extraordinary Latin American Bishops' Conference CELAM I took place in Rio de Janeiro. Its importance was in the higher levels of the church hierarchy dealing with social problems in their own continent. In 1963, a group of Chicago priests created the first Ecclesiastic Base Community in Panama, the future base for the Liberation theologians' activities. From there the idea spread to many parts of Latin America and then to the rest of the Third World. In 1967, a message emanating from 17 bishops from the Third World spoke of Christianity as the "true socialism," which the church must acknowledge by supporting the just distribution of all goods and fundamental equality. All over Latin America religious orders established centers for the study of social sciences and social action. Under the impact of Vatican II and new social analyses of Latin American society, the church underwent modernization and Latin Americanization—just at the time when developmentalism was found wanting.

In 1968 CELAM II took place in Medellín, followed in 1979 by CELAM III in Puebla, Mexico. The results of these conferences remain a matter of debate, mainly because they were trying to compromise between the more traditional and the more progressive elements among the Latin American bishops, with the consequence that both groups could find encouragement for their positions. They were, however, sufficiently clear and outspoken on the causes of many social issues and on the responsibility of the church to serve as a legitimization for those engaged in theoretical and practical innovative religious activities in Latin America.

At Medellín[2] the church overcame the tendency of separating spirituality from political reality, not by abandoning one in favor of the other, but by combining the two. The conference resolved that liberation and participation ("horizontalism") require freedom from the "institutionalized violence" of surviving internal and external colonial structures that are "seeking unbounded profits" and foment an economic dictatorship; and from the international "imperialism of money." Development that places "greater emphasis upon economic progress than on the social well-being of the people" must be rejected. For this reason, communism and capitalism, by replacing spiritual with material welfare, were an affront to human dignity.

The call went out for a theology responding to "the signs of the times." The choice was made to go out to the poor and demonstrate solidarity with them, formulated in the subsequent Puebla Conference as "the preferential option for the poor." Liberation—a concept frequently occurring in the documents—was expanded to mean freeing the poor from whoever or whatever oppressed and exploited them, for granting them participation in decisions on social affairs affecting their lives, even if they touched on religious subjects. The poor were to be included in the "collegiality" of which Vatican II was speaking in relation to the clergy. The relationship between the spiritual and the material was readily established by the argument (elaborated at Puebla) that sin was undermining human dignity, and that the prevailing social structures were sinful and in need of change.

Developing consciousness (conscientization) of their position and potentialities was suggested as the way for individuals to liberate themselves. Ecclesiastic Base Communities were praised as a means to achieve this goal. And pastoral guidance was proposed as the method by which liberation must be accomplished in the spirit of the Gospel.

Medellín, as well as later Puebla, also signaled considerable independence from Rome. They weakened the long-standing alliance between the church, governments, and the military. They eroded the colonial character of the church. They began to turn the Catholic church into a Latin American institution, committed to worldly service to society and the defense of the poor, without of course denying the fundamental tenets of the Catholic church or the ultimate authority of Rome. Pope Paul VI had set the tone of the conference by his presence and by his statement, "We wish to personify the Christ of a poor and hungry people."

The Puebla Conference did not progress further from the advanced stance assumed by the majority[3] of the bishops attending Medellín. In his opening address, the pope warned that liberation must be conceived in the Christian sense, "liberation from everything that oppresses human beings, but especially liberation from sin and the evil one, in the joy of knowing God and being known by him." Liberation could not simply be reduced to the domain of economics, politics, society, and culture.

Liberation theologians were not in disagreement. And as to horizontalism, the then Archbishop Hélder Câmara said that his cross was vertical as well as horizontal.

The conference turned out to be confirmative rather than innovative, thanks largely to intense activity by the more conservative section of the clergy and to second thoughts by some bishops about the political risks of the progressivism at Medellín. Besides, the conservative Cardinal Trujillo had become secretary of CELAM.

However, the strategy of the conservatives to use Puebla as a mute on the results of Medellín failed. The conference started again with a consideration of this world, especially the Latin American world, only thereafter to discuss its spiritual meaning and the tasks of the church. There was little comfort for them in statements such as these: "Viewing it in the light of faith, we see the growing gap between rich and poor as a scandal and a contradiction to Christian existence. The luxury of a few becomes an insult to the wretched poverty of the vast masses . . . the Church sees a situation of social sinfulness, all the more serious because it exists in countries that call themselves Catholic and are capable of changing the situation." The causes of this situation were found in economic, social, and political structures, whose extermination demands "personal conversion and profound structural changes: that will meet the people's aspirations for authentic social changes."[4] Nor could conservatives relish references to "institutionalized" injustice or to political violence supported by "totalitarian or authoritarian" governments, abusing their power and violating human rights in the name of "National Security" (the codewords in Latin America for the oppression, torture, and murder of citizens).

In spite of some ambiguity in the documents and resolutions emanating from the two conferences, there was enough content in both to serve as support and justification for the Liberation theologians, especially their activism. The "Final Document" of the Puebla Conference, for instance, proposed that Catholic education must produce the agents who will effect the permanent, organic change that Latin American society needs. There was not only awareness but deliberateness at both conferences regarding the political implications of advocating social change or dealing with secular matters. It was clear to all that making material well-being part of religious liberation necessarily would have political consequences.

The more conservative sections of the Catholic clergy shy away from political involvements. The Liberation theologians come to terms with this situation expressly by refusing to acknowledge a separation between salvation as a task for the church to achieve and material well-being as a task for the state to handle. As good Christians they will, however, insist that the ultimate, total liberation of man exceeds the powers of man and requires a gift of God. They have never denied a need for spiritual liberation and a few of them have been hesitant to advocate political action expressly. But since by the nature of things, temporal politics are unavoidable in the execution of religiously founded changes necessary to eliminate the causes of poverty (as Christ and the Bible fully recognized and accepted), the more reform-minded clergy and most Liberation theologians willingly condone political action by clergy and Catholic laymen. Covertly, of course, all sections of the church engage in political action as they have always done everywhere. Indeed, whether the position of the church is that earthly conditions must be accepted and liberation comes late in or possibly after life, or whether it is that liberation begins on earth and can partially be achieved on earth, either position has significant political aspects.

Even if, in their search for the causes of poverty, the Liberation theologians were to restrict themselves to essentially religious, theological matters, political implications could hardly be avoided. The individual's personal conversion and salvation, his relation and duty to his God, his conduct of religious life could theoretically be discussed, and have traditionally been considered, to be of concern only to the church, not the state. But as a social creature, a person's behavior—sinful or otherwise—affects the society and therewith assumes a political dimension of concern to the state.

In practice, the church has never been able to remain outside of politics. It merely tried to concentrate the handling of political matters in the Vatican. With the newer concern of the individual's total social environment, even in regard to his religious life, such monopolization is increasingly difficult. Since Vatican II, the concept of separation had to be discarded, though it lingers on in rhetoric. The official church now recognizes that undoing poverty, establishing justice, creating equality, allowing popular participation, involve governments as well as national and international politics. Reaching these goals requires power for the solution of problems no longer amenable to purely local or even national treatment.

Having to deal officially and openly with political institutions and subjects has tended to make the church uneasy ever since it had assumed a limited role in worldly affairs and became inner-directed. The more conservative wing of the church still remains uneasy about activism outside strictly religious concerns. As popes regularly pointed out, the church prefers the contemplative life over the "heresy of action" (Pope John XXIII in 1962). Or, as a document of Vatican II expressed it, the essence of the church is "that she be . . . eager to act and yet devoted to contemplation," but that the action be "directed and subordinated" to contemplation.[5]

The activism probably more than the ideas of the Liberation theologians is making the more conservative wing of the church uncomfortable and some of its leaders outright hostile. Their repugnance was only gradually being expressed openly and frankly, and then often disguisedly in theological terms. The widening of the poverty issue from the doctrinally and politically more comfortable appeal to charity on earth to the complex and controversial management of its causes and cures in this world which many encyclicals initiated and the Liberation theologians were expanding, is proving unsettling to the Catholic church and asserted to be outright dangerous by many governments. Liberation theology is no longer a purely theological matter to be fought out within the walls of the church. It is squarely also in the political arena (and it is that part with which this book is greatly concerned).

Since the older theologians and eventually the official church had already recognized the cause of poverty largely in the prevailing social structure, the Liberation theologians could proceed from there. Beginning with the capitalist system and its consequences for the working class and the poor, and essentially agreeing with the analysis of the social encyclicals, the Liberation theologians emphasize the evil effects the system had and is continuing to have on Latin America.

They see the fundamental difficulty in the traditional collusion between the upper hierarchy and the powers that be, which eventually meant a collusion between the church and the capitalists and (modern) feudalists or big landowners in Latin America. The changing attitude of the official church toward this relationship following Vatican II, Medellín and Puebla, was too recent and too limited to mean for the progressive clergy anything more than a beginning in dissolving the collusion and to undo all the consequences which the hundreds of years old collusion had for the mass of the poor people.

The Liberation theologians therefore ascribe the apathy, lack of education, acceptance of their fate as God-given by the poor to the teaching of the church over hundreds of years. This passivity enabled the oligarchies to exploit the people ruthlessly.

The system (i.e. church plus oligarchy) kept the poor subdued, making them unaware of their potential to bring about their material liberation by their own efforts. As Pope John Paul II and many Liberation theologians have pointed out, changes in the social systems of Latin America have become much more difficult since by now the capitalist system, and especially those aspects causing the poverty, are globalized. Raising the social consciousness of the poor, while in any case indispensable, is no longer sufficient. The institutions blamed for the poverty are intertwined with international institutions, including public international organizations, which the poor of Latin America (or anywhere else for that matter) cannot affect.

The globalization of the capitalist system, the official church and Liberation theologians agree, has created a new type of political and

economic dependency upon outside states and multinational corporations. The poor of Latin America have been hit with particular severity
due to the export-oriented nature of most Latin American economies. In
the view of Leonardo Boff, this international domination is now being
"extrojected" along with the dominator who has for so long kept people
in subjection and with whom the church had been associated for so long.
For this reason, the Latin American nationalism includes in its anti-
targets a "Euro-oriented Church."

One of the tools of these international capitalists, as the theologians
and some popes see it, is the system of international organizations, especially those creating stringent conditions for their assistance to the
Third World countries and then insisting upon supervising and controlling adherence by these countries. As most of them are governed by the
richer and capitalist countries, the Latin American countries find it very
difficult to organize their internal affairs with a view to ameliorating
poverty. Class conflict is seen as no longer limited to classes within countries, but is transferred to dominant versus dominated countries.
Gutiérrez therefore suggests "Only a break from the status quo, that is,
a profound transformation of the private property system, access to
power of the exploited class, and a social revolution to a new society, a
socialist society . . ." could bring about adequate change nationally and
internationally.[6]

This reference to the international connections in Liberation Theology
is not accidental. The Theology and "dependencia" theory developed to
a large degree simultaneously. It would be a gross exaggeration and ignoring the historical and intellectual roots of Liberation Theology to say
Liberation Theology was the transfer of dependencia into the ecclesiastical realm. But considerable influence of at least the spirit, that is,
nationalism, of the theory is undeniable. Gutiérrez as well as Boff and
others have spoken derogatorily of the Euro-centered Catholicism as a
cause of Latin American difficulties.

As the theologians and encyclicals recognized, the situation is aggravated by sections of the local oligarchy, "the internal colonialists," coop-
erating with the external capitalists. That is why at Medellín there was a
demand for freedom from institutionalized violence and colonial structures internally, and of freedom from the international imperialism of
money. Antonio Pérez Esclarín spoke of the idolatrous God of the
oppressors as "the God of the White conqueror, the God who expects
submission from those who are enslaved . . . the God of the colonizers
who denies humanity and equality to the colonized."[7]

The nationalism implied in these statements actually was quite open
and referred to international capitalism as well as to the official church.
It must be considered a major motor driving the Liberation theologians
and is of direct relevance to the causes of poverty as the theologians see it.

Actually, the major points of the Liberation theologians on poverty are not so entirely new. There is considerable congruency in the positions taken by several popes, some nineteenth century theologians, and the Liberation theologians on the causes of poverty. All parties claim to derive their conclusions from the Gospel. Their consensus is an important factor. But the methods by which the conclusions are reached or the conclusions themselves, become subjects of controversy when their consequences are to be translated into action, when remedies are to be found and applied.

Notwithstanding disputes among theologians, and between theologians and the church in the past, none of their positions posed real threats to existing social systems. No one made suggestions for the use of means to eliminate causes going beyond the limits established by existing social systems. Revolutionary changes in or of systems were engineered by outsiders, not the church or the theologians. This situation may change now when the theologians implant the idea in the poor masses' minds that the key to improving their lives lies in changing the structures supporting their exploitation and oppression to which they themselves can contribute (conscientization!).

This innovation proves embarrassing to the church because Liberation theologians deduce their ideas from the Gospel; justify their "worldly" Theology with a reinterpretation of the Bible; base their theological ideology upon Latin American history and conditions; build the "church of the poor" upon the experience of the poor. In brief, the church is embarrassed when the theologians are trying to anchor their social analysis and the treatment of poverty in the Gospel making them part of church doctrine and Magisterium, while Rome is partly or totally in disagreement with the theologians.

Another innovation is to let deeds follow their words—quite in line with the admonition of the Gospel, but also making some church circles nervous. The criticism of the theologians that they have so far failed to develop a comprehensive statement of their Theology, an alternative social system, or methods for generating one, is justified to some extent. But more than anyone before them, they are attempting to promote and provoke action based upon the discovery of the causes of poverty. Without implementation by action, an analysis of the causes of poverty would be little more than an intellectual exercise. This determination to draw the practical consequences of the analysis is, in fact, the foundation for the opposition the theologians have encountered from many different quarters. Their activism, in contrast to that of the clergy, religious, and laypersons of the past, is more intense and socially more consequential. For this reason, mainly, it is considered by those who are disadvantageously affected politically dangerous and taken so seriously.

6
Implications of Remedies for Poverty

The choice and effectiveness of remedies for poverty are influenced by the political environment and the capabilities of those applying them. The nineteenth century church was not well situated in the politics of the day to go beyond harmless tradition. It was hindered by weightier troubles than pauperism and poverty. Only in the twentieth century the spotty development of a social conscience among some Latin American governments and the birth of Liberation Theology enabled or forced it to take a more outspoken stand on the problem of poverty.

In the nineteenth century the official church was, in general, fighting for its survival, first as a worldly and a spiritual power, later only as a spiritual power. The threat came from new political forces and from new ideologies. The church's inclination was to oppose both, preferably to restore earlier conditions which had allowed it to be a spiritual and a temporal power. As a minimum it aimed at maintaining the status quo. It succeeded only minimally, and at the cost of being branded reactionary.

This tendency of the church to preserve conditions under which it could exist more or less satisfactorily continued into the twentieth century. In Latin America in so far as the situation there was comparable to that in nineteenth century Europe, the church again, until at least Medellín, was in close liaison (and to a great extent still is) with the ruling oligarchies. It was a comfortable position, in spite of many conflicts. There was no point in disturbing it gratuitously. While the church was rhetorically advocating many changes in many places, it had concretely been doing very little about them.

As the numerous encyclicals emphasizing the need for social change appeared, the church never threatened to try to translate them into reality. Instead, it acquiesced passively in the perpetuation of the conditions causing the misery of the masses. Even in countries where Liberation Theology is relatively strong, very large sections of the clergy, among them members high in the hierarchy and the lay public, retain the old tendency of staying with the powers that be until the last moment, either out of apathy or sympathy—notwithstanding the role the church recently played in the overthrow of several governments.

During the history of the last two hundred years at least, the church certainly has been deeply involved at times in world politics. But the issues were quite different from those agitating the church now as a result of the arrival of the Liberation theologians, who are themselves one of the "signs of the times." Those issues had to do mainly with the relations between church and state, who was to control whom, to what degree and in what respects. Or they had to do with contrast and conflict between a spiritually minded church and a materialist-minded middle class in the urban centers. They were not focused on poverty and social justice, not on the status or behavior of ruling oligarchies, not on fundamentals of internal national political and social systems. They dealt safely with politically less sensitive matters. They did not involve changes in the system. They rarely threatened worldly powers. In the many disputes between the church and the urban middle class, the quarrels within the clergy or between the pro- and anticlerics, in the tensions arising forever in political-ecclesiastic relations, the poor masses in the countryside and later in the cities were the forgotten people.

The Liberation theologians have two characteristics interfering with the fundamental modus vivendi of church and state in Latin America. They favor radical and speedy social change. More specifically they oppose the very system in which the church has either been allied or coexisted with its supporters. And—in contrast to their nineteenth century European predecessors—they are not satisfied with rhetoric or superficial improvements through repairs which could easily be controlled by Rome or fit into existing political systems. They are (or support) activists who will sooner or later produce the structural changes found necessary by popes and theologians. Although the official church tends to think otherwise, the theologians, however, are not advocating activities outside the framework of the church. On the contrary, most insist upon working as good Catholics and within the framework of the church. This loyalty contributes little to their popularity with high church officials for both ecclesiastic and secular political reasons. They would be easier to handle if they represented a small sect outside the mainstream of the church and its politics, so that the church could dissociate itself from them.

With respect to capabilities of transforming ideas into practice, the power of the official church places it in a more favorable position than a small group of activists. Yet, the very basis of this power, the vast geographic expanse of the Catholic church across a great variety of cultures, dictates caution in its undertakings. The risks could be particularly acute in connection with poverty and social justice. Any change affecting existing conditions involves a large dose of public policies and politics. Measures taken by the church could potentially antagonize a greater circle of followers than smaller groups could; or they could antagonize some groups, but not others. It has to tread more carefully than either individuals or national churches. Within the limits of the hierarchical order, the church has therefore recognized the "extremely wise norm" that local clergy "must take into account the circumstances which obtain in different areas and nations" (*Princeps pastorum,* 1959 no. 16).

One could assume that this rule works both ways. Measures initiated in Rome would have to be adapted to local conditions. But also measures initiated locally, judged useful and within the Magisterium, should be supported by Rome. But when the Liberation theologians applied this principle by attempting to accommodate the Gospel to Latin American conditions, little support came from Rome in either weighty or light matters. In many respects, the official church even showed hostility. Yet the spread of Liberation Theology and of Ecclesiastic Base Communities in the Third World exposed the limits of the church's power, just as it was unable to control the nineteenth century progressive theologians, criticizing and Indexing notwithstanding. The "circumstances which obtain in different areas and nations," in other words, must not only affect ideas originating in Rome. Rome will sometimes have to adapt to those coming from different areas of the world!

Religious concern with poverty should be more than preaching, as many encyclicals agree. The church must do more than acknowledge its existence, at the risk of political complications, if it wants to be relevant, if it does not want to repeat the "scandal" of the nineteenth century and this time lose the masses of the Third World. But the official church is always worried about political risks, more likely involved in material than spiritual liberation. They could make the church the savior of the poor in the Third World. But they could also get into conflict with governments and lessen the church's political influence. In such a dilemma, the church traditionally chose caution. Perhaps not too surprisingly, therefore, the Liberation theologians are often criticized for giving precedence to material over spiritual welfare. Though this criticism is expressed in theological terms, the political motivation is transparent.

In the pre-social-encyclical age, such criticism might have been understandable—because, luckily for the church, it could then be justified on theological grounds. The church was legitimately not interested in anything more than giving alms and shelter. In this mentality, Leo XIII's astonishment can be understood: What "especially excites our surprise" is that in speaking of rewards and punishments during the last judgment "Christ omits those works of mercy which comfort the soul and [is] referring only to those which comfort the body" (*Graves de communi re,* 1902 no. 14). It took time before the official church unequivocally accepted the notion of relief from earthly misery as part of total liberation. When it did, this dual character of liberation (spiritual and material) became one of the marks distinguishing Catholicism from Marxism. For Marxism ends with material liberation; Catholicism begins with material liberation as an important step toward spiritual liberation.

Once this concept of total liberation had been accepted, the church had to define the relationship between material and spiritual liberation. This had to be done for theological reasons because total liberation meant expanding theology and Magisterium—and for political reasons, in order to calm fears of political dangers threatening from venturing into Caesar's realm.

Leo XIII placed both liberations on the same level when he said, "To the teachings which enjoin a twofold charity of spiritual and corporal works Christ adds his own example, so that no one may fail to recognize the importance which he attaches to it" (*Graves de communi re,* 1901 no. 15). Sixty years later, John XXIII reconfirmed: "For the teaching of Christ joins, as it were, earth with heaven, in that it embraces the whole man, namely his soul and body" (*Mater et magistra,* 1961 no. 2).

Not many popes were as unambiguous. Yet in the light of their pronouncements, it is difficult to understand the criticism of Liberation theologians in the Sacred Congregation for the Doctrine of the Faith's *Instruction on Certain Aspects of the "Theology of Liberation"* (1984), VI-4) that they are tempted "to reduce the Gospel to an earthly gospel." There was no fundamental disagreement with most popes of the twentieth century on material liberation; there were only different emphases, different priorities.

Leo XIII had stated in 1884 (*Humanum genus,* no. 29) that poverty should be relieved "as far as possible." His message in *Graves de communi re* 1901 no. 6, was that Christian democracy "must provide for better conditions for the masses, with the ulterior object of promoting the perfection of souls made for eternal things." Rescue of the poor "should, of course, be solicitous first for the eternal good of souls, but it must not neglect what is good and helpful in life," he states in the same encyclical (No. 13). In the course of time, this relationship between spiritual and material liberation was repeated more and more frequently, and more explicitly because "often souls are not reached except through the relief of corporal misery and economic needs" (*Nos es muy conocida,*

1937 no. 13). John Paul II finally supported the concept of complete, total liberation as outlined in the Sacred Congregation for the Doctrine of the Faith's *Instruction on Christian Freedom and Liberation*, 1986. With this development of the church in outspoken support of advocating something more than alms giving, it had taken the final step. Its power now backed the concept. The Liberation theologians no longer were alone. The gap between them and the church on this point was closed. The influence Liberation theologians already had in Latin America and other parts of the Third World was enhanced by the addition of the official church's power. But serious differences remained about the remedies advocated by each, or, perhaps better, about the methods by which the remedies were to be applied. With both agreeing that the social system is a root of the evil, the manner of change then becomes a matter of political action, beyond the bailiwick of theology. For this reason, conscientization is suspect to the official church. Occasional signs of welcome by Pope John Paul II and some high members of the hierarchy remain outweighed by opposition. Local theologians and members of the Ecclesiastic Base Communities still have to fend for themselves. The protective power of the church does not extend so far.

7
The Remedies
of the Church

After acceptance by the church of social structures as the cause of poverty, it had to adapt its approach to the solution of the problem. Pope Leo XIII, in *Dall'alto dell'apostolico seggio,* 1890 no. 17, showed the way. "The social questions which now so greatly occupy men's mind would find their way to the best and most complete solution, by the practical application of the gospel precepts of charity and justice." The demand for conversion began the adaptation, uncontroversially enough. It remained thereafter forever one of the steps toward a solution. Conversion would introduce charity and justice into the daily lives of humans, whatever else needed to be done.

Obviously, conversion was not an innovation, nor did it remain the only suggested solution. But initially, the church hesitated to go further, partly in the belief that conversion would immediately improve the fate of the poor. For a long time, conversion became the almost panacean solution to earthly problems. *Rerum novarum,* 1891 no. 28, asserted "Christian morality, when adequately and completely practiced, leads of itself to temporal prosperity, for it merits the blessing of God, who is the source of all blessings." With conversion would come just wages, decent living conditions, a share of all in social amenities, humanization of labor, ownership of land, participation in enterprises for all. "If you truly love the laborer (and you must love him because his conditions of life approach nearer to those of the Divine Master), you must assist him materially and religiously," prescribed Pope Pius XI in *Nos es muy conocida,* 1937 no. 16.

This task was found to be difficult. The prospect for achievement was bleak. Pope Pius XI, in *Divini redemptoris,* 1937 no. 50, and after him other popes, complainted bitterly that "the manner of acting in certain Catholic circles has done much to shake the faith of the working-classes in the religion of Jesus Christ." If Catholics as "Christian employers and industrialists" could not be converted, how much more difficult would it be to convert non-Catholics. The discouraging record notwithstanding, the intervention of religion and the church were considered indispensable to generate the social changes. This conviction did not prevent questions from arising that could not be answered by reference to conversion and salvation.

How could conversion produce modifications in the capitalist system when the church considered as "natural" two of its fundamental elements: private property and the existence of classes?

On private property, the church was softening its rigid stand over the last 150 years. In 1849, Pope Pius IX, in *Nostis et nobiscum,* no. 32, had still denied that the property of others "can be taken and divided or in some other way turned to the use of everyone." Subsequent encyclicals gradually modified this absolute position. By 1931, *Quadragesimo anno,* no. 48, declared "either the right to property itself or its use, that is, the exercise of ownership, is circumscribed by the necessities of social living." In 1981, John Paul II's *Laborem exercens,* no. 14, elaborated that under certain circumstances "one cannot exclude the *socialization,* in suitable conditions, of certain means of production"—one form of his "social mortgage" on property.

The church was obviously reluctant to draw a clear-cut line between private right to property and a social claim upon property. Occasional fairly specific references to limitations on the right did not solve the problem. Either they had very narrow discrete situations in view or they were hedged in by objectively undefinable conditions. *Gaudium et spes,* 1965 no. 69, for instance, specified that "in extreme necessity" a person had the right to procure for himself what he needed out of the riches of others. In 1967 *Populorum progressio,* no. 24, asserted that the "common good" sometimes demanded "expropriation." Both encyclicals, later others, and Pope John Paul II during his travels in the Third World, referred to the need to distribute uncultivated lands, possibly through expropriation, to make them fruitful, if the owners would not do it.

On the existence of classes, the official church had much to say, but little to propose. This was merely an indication that it found this to be a very troublesome problem for which it had no realistic solution fitting its principles. *Rerum novarum,* 1891 nos. 19, 21, 22, 28, 45, had already explained that assuming necessary hostility between classes was a mistake. Nature had ordained "that the two classes should dwell in harmony and agreement." To achieve this happy state, Christian institutions should be introduced, for there is "no intermediary more powerful than religion . . . in drawing the rich and the working classes together, by reminding each of its duties to the other, and especially to the obligation of justice." Besides, the argument continued, compared to eternal happiness, temporal riches and poverty make no difference. Each side should be satisfied with keeping up its conditions of life "becomingly," no more, no less (at another time, the workers were conceded only a "frugal" existence as adequate). If those Christian principles would prevail, "the respective classes will not only be united in bonds of friendship, but also those of brotherly love." *Tametsi futura prospicientibus,* 1900 no. 12, repeated, "The strife between the classes and masses will die away; mutual rights will be respected. If Christ be listened to, both rich and poor will do their duty."

The version of Pope Benedict XV in *Ad beatissimi,* 1914 no. 13, was:

Brotherly love is not calculated to get rid of the differences of conditions and therefore of classes—a result which is just as impossible as that in the living body all the members should have the same functions and dignity—but it will bring it to pass that those who occupy higher positions will in some way bring themselves down to those in a lower position, and treat them not only justly, for it is only right that they should, but kindly and in a friendly and patient spirit, and the poor on their side will rejoice in their prosperity and rely confidently on their help—even as the younger son of a family relies on the help and protection of his elder brother.

Succeeding popes continued to show the same confidence in people, but not in the disappearance of classes or conflict between them. Pope John Paul II struggled at length with the problem in *Laborem exercens,* 1981, without coming to a definite conclusion. The existence of employers and of labor unions was accepted as a fact. But he advocated that they should share means of work, profits, management, and so on to preserve the dignity of labor and the person of the laborers and to avoid class war. Class struggle, he pointed out, should not be one class against another. It should be a joint struggle for social justice leading to community and solidarity between all the members of the society and to the common good. Labor unions and legitimate strikes should not aim at securing special benefits for just one class of people, but at establishing the common welfare when disturbed by improper action of employers or managers. In 1986, the *Instruction on Christian Freedom and Liberation,* no. 77, reconfirmed that church approval of labor unions did not imply class struggle as "the structural dynamism of social life." But it proposed no better alternative than "a noble and reasoned struggle for justice and solidarity." "The Christian will always prefer the path of dialogue and joint action."

In 1988, *Sollicitudo rei socialis,* no. 43, stated, "The motivating concern for the poor . . . must be translated at all levels into concrete actions, until it decisively attains a series of necessary reforms. Each local situation will show what reforms are most urgent and how they can be achieved." If, in this last sentence, the pope had the Latin American situation in mind, one can only wonder how the pacifist position on clashes of interest between classes could be reconciled with it.

In the light of the police state methods prevalent in so many Latin American and other countries, the exploitive habits of employers and the ruthless practices of big landowners even still today, the very optimistic position of the church on class war is neither convincing nor promising. The church's generous confidence in people is difficult to reconcile with encyclicals complaining about the inadequacy of conversion and the constantly growing inequalities within and between nations.

With the problems of private property and class conflict believed to have been solved, the church could devote itself more intensely to developing the plan for a social system in which the evils of poverty and injustice would disappear. True to characteristic conservatism, it proved to be more critical of existing systems or new proposals than inventive. This was perhaps also due to approval of any system whatsoever reflecting the values of the church. Pope Pius XI had written, in *Ubi arcano Dei consilio,* 1922 no. 12, when he referred to evils arising from political party conflicts, that the Catholic faith was easily reconcilable "with any reasonable and just system of government."

Capitalism and socialism were found wanting at an early date. Both were dominated by intolerable materialism. Capitalism was found guilty of creating poverty and inequality, socialism, of denying private property, and advocating class war. Pope John Paul II in his encyclical *Sollicitudo rei socialis,* 1988 no. 41, made very clear this stance of the church was not equivalent to a third position. Actually, the church did not really have one, nor propose one. Rather, the church's critique of capitalism and socialism was intended to highlight the moral inadequacy of both systems.

Several popes had affirmed that analysis of society and making blueprints for a desirable social system were not the church's mission. Yet, since 1891 its critique of existing systems and outline of desirable social features amounted, in fact, to a "social policy" with very broadly implied features of a desirable society.

The foundation was to be association or its more modern equivalent of community and solidarity. The fundamental goal was to create peaceful societies in which conflict was to be replaced by cooperation. Employers as well as laborers in industry and agriculture were to form associations to facilitate cooperation. Initially, some paternalism was noticeable in these proposals because employers were granted a slightly favored position. By the end of the nineteenth century, the church had reconciled itself to the existence of independent labor unions, but never quite renounced the idea of corporations and guilds.

At the beginning of the 1930s, the continuing struggle between the classes led to the demand for an alternative system dealing more peacefully with poverty and injustice. Along with the trend of the times, much talk of a "new order" could be heard. In *Quadragesimo anno,* 1931 no. 88, Pope Pius XI opted for social reform. After strongly indicting unrestrained competition, he concluded "the right ordering of economic life cannot be left to a free competition of forces." Loftier principles of justice and charity should prevail. What institutions this would need, neither he nor any of his successors ever spelled out.

In 1939, Pius XII's *Summi pontificatus* argued for changes to meet popular needs. He then declared it the solemn duty of the church, in *Fidei donum,* 1957 no. 21, to give Africans a "new world order" to rescue them from their unfortunate situation. Later popes expanded that duty to everybody.

In 1961, *Mater et magistra,* no. 23, once again appealed to laborers and employers to "regulate their mutual relations in a spirit of human solidarity and in accordance with the bond of Christian brotherhood" for neither the unregulated competition of capitalism nor the class struggle in the Marxist sense were compatible with Christian principles. Pope John Paul II's 1988 encyclical then summarized these various step by step expansions of the church's social doctrine, all leading eventually to a global community and solidarity.

The problem became to find agencies able and willing to transform these proposals into practice, since the church itself considers implementation beyond its mission. The church's aim is to direct behavior. The church engages in "a careful reflection on the complex realities of human existence . . . in the light of faith and of the Church's tradition," declared John Paul II's 1988 encyclical, no. 41. The result belongs to theology, not ideology. Considering the minimum outline of any social system allowing for free play of Catholic values, the task to create one is formidable. The church assigns it to itself, lay associations, and the state.

The prerogative of the church is to achieve personal conversion, generally be in charge of defining moral principles for personal and public life, supervise the adherence of Catholic organizations to Catholic principles, and invoke the help of the state in the secular task of maintaining a social order reflecting Christian values (cf. *Redemptor hominis,* 1979 nos. 12, 17). Since moral values permeate all human behavior, this role of the church would give it influence upon private and public life, including the alleviation of poverty and injustice. At the same time, this high position as moral arbiter would enable the church to be a critic of social action without getting involved in it. It would avoid splits within the church and maintain the separation of religious from secular matters.

The prerequisite for the church remaining aloof from social action would be freedom of action for the executive lay agencies. It existed in most of Europe when this model was developed. It certainly does not exist in many parts of the Third World.[1] There the church, against its wish, is obliged to become actively involved in secular matters to enforce its moral principles, with, especially in Latin America, exactly the consequences it had always feared: a breakdown of unity within the church.

The Catholic lay associations the church chose to execute its policies were not as submissive as it probably expected. Quite often, they objected to serve merely as tools of the church, insisting upon their own interpretations of what action was needed in given cases. They tended to develop their own identity. In other situations they were suppressed by governments. Occasionally, the church found it impossible to preserve the strictly Catholic character of an organization, for instance a labor union or a cooperative. Many times the church had to come to terms with the fact that its monopoly of dealing with poverty had ceased, so that Catholic and non-Catholic agencies began to cooperate on a secular plane more than the church found desirable.

One of the agencies to serve as an executive for Catholic principles is the Catholic parties. While they never were secular appendices of the church (less and less so in fact as democratization in parts of the world advanced), their programs reflected at least the essence of Catholic social doctrine. They enable an individual to be simultaneously a faithful member of the universal church and a good citizen in regional political processes. They are a good channel to political power in nations where a party system prevails. In the Third World, all too often parties represent merely narrow elites so that the usefulness of Catholic or Christian Democratic parties are severely limited.

A further reduction of the parties' usefulness was their loss of distinctiveness. Their platform was duplicated or preempted by other, especially socialist, parties as the social welfare state arrived.[2] The church and the Catholic parties had no special alternative to offer, distinguishing them in the social field from other institutions and parties. As, moreover, Catholic parties were in many respects conservative while other parties were more progressive and aggressive, many Catholic voters could give their votes to these secular parties without betraying their Catholic moral principles. Sometimes, on the contrary, the failure of the church in many countries to dissolve alliances with the most conservative sections of the ruling groups, a Catholic conscience would drive voters to secular radical parties as better qualified to produce social change than the Catholic parties. This, in turn, added the difficulty from the standpoint of the church that the leaders of these parties disagreed with the church. They built their own power base within the party, ignoring or even rejecting suggestions coming from the church.

Another major agency is Catholic Action. It has had a checkered career in regard both to its nature and its relationship with the church. It started out during the nineteenth century as one of the many Catholic associations of the most diverse kind which proliferated when political and social conditions in Europe facilitated the growth of nongovernmental organizations and associations. They had national, regional, or local scope. They varied in character from place to place and over time. The one stable factor, whether they were political parties, workers' associations, educational institutions, charitable organizations, or social clubs, was their Catholic orientation. Even this ranged from overemphasis and exclusiveness ("ghettoization"!) to underemphasis and openness regarding Catholic membership.[3] They also covered a broad spectrum politically, from conservatism to progressivism. But the raison d'être of all was the advancement of Catholic social doctrine or its realization.

Gradually, Catholic Action outgrew other organizations in importance and became something like an umbrella organization with a presence in almost all parts of the world. The church singled it out as of great usefulness and gave it special attention. It played a significant role in the attempt to apply social doctrine in all aspects of daily life. It was, like all other executive agencies of the church, composed exclusively of laypersons. Pius XI defined Catholic Action as the "participation of the laity in the apostolate of the Church's hierarchy." Catholic Action would be a federation of individual movements, each helping to spread the Magisterium among the laity. The "devotion of Catholics to comfort and elevate the mass of the people is in keeping with the spirit of the Church and is most comfortable to the examples which the Church has always held up for imitation" said Pope Leo XIII (*Graves de communi re,* 1901 no. 18).

In response to the Social Question, Catholic Action expanded activities from philanthropy to almost anything that could lighten the burden on the workers and would help them to improve their situation. This included action toward social change. But when this action expanded into the political arena or when it was shared with non-Catholics, the church would not hesitate to forbid the action or the entire particular organization (e.g. Opera dei Congressi, 1904, in Italy; Sillan in France, 1910; French "worker-priests" after World War II; an activist group in Argentina). This restriction upon the activities of Catholic Action made it difficult to work for social change, even when high members of the clergy suggested it (as was the case in France under Cardinal Saliège in Toulouse in 1945). Such censorship by the church raised the question in Rome of the relationship between the church and Catholic Action, and the same question in the minds of the members of Catholic Action.

The answer from the church was not always the same. Some popes insisted upon a much tighter control over the activities of Catholic Action

than others. Leo XIII seemed quite unconcerned about the organization of Catholic Action or the church's control over it. Other popes
insisted on strict supervision and guidance by the church, and even a
mandate for Catholic Action or any of its participating organizations
from a local bishop (e.g. *Il fermo proposito,* 1905 no. 11; *Pieni l'animo,*
1906 no. 11; *Singulari quadam,* 1912 nos. 4, 8; *Princeps pastorum,* 1959
no. 28).

The members of Catholic Action are not very happy with the strict
control of the church. They want to be more than the militant arm of the
church. Moreover, they argued, they have the advantage over the church
of being able to adjust more quickly to the demands of new situations. To
quote the *New Catholic Encyclopaedia* (article "Catholic Action"), if
"the mark of the authentic layman is a spirit of discovery and autonomy
in lay life, issuing from competence based upon the development of his
natural talents, it is difficult to see how this ministry can be conceived as
an extension of the clerical or hierarchical church."

The issue came to a head during Vatican II, 1965. Five days were
devoted to a discussion of the Decree on the Apostolate of the Laity.
While some observers felt a liberalization of Catholic Action activities
was the result, a close reading of the decree in conjunction with the new
Code of Canon Law hardly bears out such an interpretation. Catholic
Action remains under the "direction," "ecclesiastical control," "church
vigilance," "church authority" of the clergy. The practical meaning of
this relationship is that Catholic Action cannot work toward bringing
about social change to help the poor any more than the official church
allows. The fact, in other words, of the church possessing a "militant
arm" does not necessarily signify action in execution of the church's
social doctrine.

There can be little doubt that Rome's treatment of Catholic Action is
one consequence of its jealously guarded hierarchical organization and
central control This is particularly true when, as in the case of Catholic
Action, activities approach the political sphere. Like Catholic Action,
Catholic political parties have experienced the same fate before and the
Liberation theologians are experiencing it now. The common ground of
these "rebellious" groups is their impatience, for one reason or another,
with the cautious and slow manner of the official church in drawing the
consequences of its own rhetoric that the abatement of poverty and
social justice requires action, albeit sometimes politically risky action,
and requires it now.

The third agency for executing the church's social doctrine is the state.
Changing social structures is a political act, representing a dilemma for
an "unpolitical" church. Many encyclicals have dealt with it. *Quadragesimo anno,* 1931 no. 80, detailed the role assigned to the state. "The
supreme authority of the state ought . . . to let the subordinate groups

handle matters and concerns of lesser importance, which would otherwise dissipate its efforts greatly. Thereby the state will more freely, powerfully, and effectively do all those things that belong to it alone, because it alone can do them: watching, urging, restraining, as occasion requires and necessity demands."

The assumption is often repeated that the state shares with the church its high principles (*Ubi arcano*, 1922 no. 65). Indeed,

as Our great predecessor, Leo XIII, wisely taught in the encyclical 'Immortale Dei', it was the Creator's will that civil sovereignty should regulate social life after the dictates of an order changeless in its universal principles; should facilitate the attainment in the temporal order, by individuals, of physical, intellectual and moral perfection; and should aid them to reach their supernatural end. Hence it is the noble prerogative and function of the State to control, aid and direct the private and individual activities of national life that they converge harmoniously towards the common good" (*Summi pontificatus* 1939, p. 25, St. Paul Editions).

Because the encyclical *Pacem in terris,* 1963, endowed the "common good" in the modern era with worldwide dimensions, Pope John XXIII called for the creation of a public authority on a global scale. Pope John Paul II in *Laborem exercens,* 1981 no. 17, followed up this request by appealing to various international organizations to use their influence toward achieving "full respect for the workers' rights, since the rights of the human person are the key element in the whole of the social order." In his *Sollicitudo rei socialis,* 1988 no. 43, he proposed several changes to restore an international balance in the service of that global common good. The state was reminded in *Pacem in terris,* 1963 no. 56, "Considerations of justice and equity . . . can at times demand that those involved in civil government give more attention to the less able to defend their rights and assert their legitimate claims." Social legislation, especially if it benefits the poor, should be conscientiously applied.

There was never any doubt about the role of the church to inspire the state with its high principles and to supervise their application. But there was controversy among Catholics concerning how the state might use its influence to solve the problems of the working class, poverty and inequality. Should the free market be maintained at all cost? Should the state intervene only to curb excesses? Should the state enforce social justice by any means? By the time *Rerum novarum,* 1891, appeared, and without any further debate after capitalism was found wanting, the choice was for state intervention.

This decision did not solve one other problem. What if the state does not play its assigned role, or, worse, if it acts contrary to church principles? The problem may not seem very acute in the First World, but it is of foremost importance in the Third World, where it has much to do with the popularity of Liberation Theology.

The answer was simple and logical. If the state denied church principles and cannot be convinced to repent, it had sinned, forfeited its authority, and relieved the citizen from his duty to obey. In *Diuturnum illud,* 1881 no. 20, Leo XIII praised the passive resistance and martyrdom of the early Christian soldiers when they were asked to break the laws of God. In *Immortale Dei,* 1885 no. 18, 32, 35, he pointed out the citizens' obedience was a duty because the government applied truth and justice to its laws, aimed at securing the common good, making obedience not a servitude but "submission to the will of God." But, by implication, misgovernment withdrew the foundation of the citizens' duty to obey. In 1888, the pope repeated this principle in *Libertas,* no. 13, "But where the power to command is wanting, or where the law is enacted contrary to reason, or to the eternal law, or to some ordinance of God, obedience is unlawful, lest, while obeying man, we may become disobedient to God." Pope John XXIII, basing his argument on Acts 5:29, said in *Pacem in terris,* 1963 no. 51, that commands contrary to God's order cannot bind a citizen's conscience "since God has more right to be obeyed than man." The *Instruction on Christian Freedom and Liberation,* 1986 no. 79, explicitly proposes passive resistance as a way "more comfortable to moral principles and having no less prospect of success" than violence.

But *Populorum progressio,* 1967 no. 31, and again that same *Instruction,* no. 79, go further. They permit armed struggle "where there is manifest, long-standing tyranny which would do great damage to fundamental personal rights and dangerous harm to the common good of the country."

These references to permissible violence are not as stunning as they may seem. First, since the Middle Ages the church had tolerated rebellion, though often hesitatingly and always as a last resort. Catholic insurgents in many violent rebellions have claimed the defense of Catholicism as one of their motivations—in the Vendée 1793, Ireland 1789, Belgium 1798, Tyrol 1808, Belgium 1830, Switzerland 1847.[4] Some clergy participated in the great French Revolution. Secondly, the contingency permitting disobedience or violence is so carefully circumscribed as never likely to occur. In any case, the church, as the guardian of the highest principles, retains the right to define at what point all relevant conditions are fulfilled.

The remedies for poverty proposed by the church appear mild as well as vague. Greater morality in public and private life are unquestionably desirable. But the call for community, solidarity, and the socially responsible use of private property with a simultaneous rejection of those socialist features most likely to achieve these ends, appears puzzling, even to churchmen. It appears all the more puzzling as many of the ends suggested in recent encyclicals coincide with those suggested by socialism.

Equally puzzling appears the resistance of the church to governments holding the better promise for changes in sinful structures than many of those, especially in the Third World, with whom the official church is in collusion. It is difficult to avoid the impression that the official church is still affected by a remnant of the mentality prevailing in the middle of the last century, when *Nostis et nobiscum,* 1849 no. 18, stated that the leaders, "whether communist or socialist, share the common aim of keeping the workers and the men of lower orders in a state of continual agitation and gradually habituating them to ever more criminal acts."

There is an irreconcilability between some of the progressive, almost socialist rhetoric in encyclicals and the still frequent cooperation between large sections of the hierarchy and very conservative oligarchies in many countries. To the masses of the poor there, socialism is not devilish and the image of the church is not of the guardian of a humanitarian law and order. As long as that image lasts, Christianity will lose "almost all the creative value of the social revolution that is embedded in her own doctrine," writes Peter J. Riga.[5]

That the church could do little more than aim at conversion of sinful people, provide guidance for highly moral behavior, and call on states to help it achieve its aims rested in the nature of its traditional doctrine, organization, and means. But since it has now chosen to enter into some very detailed analyses of social evils, it can hardly avoid a corresponding duty to suggest its social structures designed to eliminate the evils it found. The least one might expect is that it give free rein to those who are trying to bring about change in the spirit of Catholicism. The Liberation theologians have shown that more than appeals, some activism in conformity with the Bible is possible. Yet they are personae non gratae in wide circles of the hierarchy.

The broader question is whether the undefined structural changes demanded by the church can be brought about by states now controlled by the very people against whom the changes are directed. The erection of new structures preventing sinful people from continuing their sinful behavior might better be left to those now suffering from the sinful structures. Nowhere, however, does the church discuss specific means beyond education by which those intended to benefit most from the changes could participate in their own liberation. The paternalism characteristic of the age of alms still influences the thinking of the official church.

8
The Remedies of the Nineteenth Century Theologians

The recognition by nineteenth century theologians, clergy, and laypersons of the causes of poverty led them to advocate remedies early. Summarizing their thoughts and actions is difficult. They worked as individuals or small groups of diverse political and economic persuasions. They were also differently affected by the intellectual ferment, the political events, and the internal church conflicts of their times. The complex interaction of these factors resulted in a great variety of views and proposals. Nevertheless, similarities in the general nature of their suggestions and activities allow some categorization.

Many were determined activists. They all believed Christianity offered and demanded solutions to the poverty problem. They did not trouble much about theological justification—though sometimes enough to have their writings placed on the Index. Nor did they greatly worry about distinguishing spiritual from material liberation. They devoted themselves mainly to the material side since the church took care of the spiritual. Their collective impact was evident in the eventual appearance of the social encyclicals. Virtually their entire substance could be traced to the thoughts of these nineteenth century theologians and religious laypersons.

There was near unanimity among them on charity. A burst of activities created hospitals, shelters, alms-giving and charitable organizations.

Conservatives among these people showed some nostalgia for the quieter times of the prerevolutionary age they were hoping to restore. Some progressives rejected charity altogether as demeaning. Others differed on mainly two points. Should charity be a private or a state function? And how should charity—recognized as insufficient—be implemented by what other remedies?

The advocates of public charity were immediately accused of Marxism and as taking the first step toward socialism. The other group, even while agitating for social changes, founded institutions to help the poor along fairly traditional lines, hence their works did not arouse opposition. Frédéric Ozanam, for instance, created the Society of St. Vincent de Paul; the Abbé Lowenbruck the Society of St. Joseph.

In Germany, charity as a remedy was advocated later than in France, but became more popular (and was soon nicknamed "romanticism"). Some Germans looked back to medieval times, dreaming of guilds and corporations (Ritter von Buss, Franz Hitze). Others considered such a reversal at best a subsidiary means to be implemented by more fundamental, modern, and radical ones. Both groups were opposed by the "integrationalists" and "maximalists" who saw the only solution in the creation of a totally Catholic society.

Similar divisions of opinion existed in other parts of Europe. But everywhere, charity continued to play a part in the search for answers to the Social Question and continues to do so today. Its popularity, however, greatly decreased over time as social security systems of various kinds, private and public, provided a more reliable means of support for the poor. There was, moreover, no illusion among large numbers of concerned individuals since poverty was due to the capitalist structure of society, charity would at best be a palliative.

Charity was replaced in prominence by association as a remedy. It became almost a panacea. "Association! That ought to be the powerful lever of modern society," wrote *Ere Nouvelle* in 1849. "Association is the true formula of social Christianity," exclaimed the *Revue Nationale* in 1848. J.-B.-H. Lacordaire saw in association based upon work and religion the only guarantee against "the continual recurrence of revolution."[1] Just who was to associate was not always clear. Most of the time workers and capitalists were envisaged. The role of the church was to exert moral influence, that of the state control over excesses. From this point onwards, however, there were many different opinions on the form and function of associations.

One group, mostly in Germany and Austria (with some adherents in France), was looking to association for the restoration of prerevolutionary-type guilds (K. von Vogelsang, W. von Ketteler, Ch. de Montalambert, J.-B.-H. Lacordaire and, in the 20th century, Austrian Chancellor Dollfuss, some Christian Democratic parties in Latin America). Among their considerations was that the lowest class had little ability to rule itself. *Graves de communi re* agreed when, in 1901 no. 8, it stated the upper class "are of the greatest use in preserving and perfecting the commonwealth."

Increasing industrialization made this remedy clearly anachronistic, and Mussolini gave corporatism a bad reputation, but the idea remains conspicuous under a variety of names (community, solidarity, etc.).

Another group was instrumental in creating workers' associations, predecessors to Catholic labor unions. Their character and function, however, became controversial. Some individuals suggested they should join with management, either to manage their enterprises or to replace workers' wages with shares in profits. Others proposed worker ownership of the tools of production. Yet others wanted to turn the associations into cooperatives to eliminate private owners and middlemen. Still others, finally, proposed purely professional worker organizations to advance the status of workers through education, training, health measures, insurance, protection of rights, and so on. The common end of all these proposals was to provide safeguards against the detrimental effects of the capitalist system upon the physical and economic welfare of the workers, but also to provide means for the workers to improve their status by their own efforts.

There was a widespread and general concern to promote education for personal and professional benefit. The church lent help by suggesting education of the clergy in social affairs. It was felt that the lack of educational opportunities for the workers facilitated their exploitation. Education, so the argument ran, would make the workers aware of their rights, their own strength, their ability to participate in politics and their entitlement to share in government (an early case of "conscientization"!). Consequently, many of those who agreed used every political device to provide education for the workers.

A dilemma was envisaged, however. Raising the status of the workers in a capitalist system might sharpen class conflict. Yet violence was condemned as un-Christian. The alternative was to be mediation by the church, a proposal which also had approval from Christian Socialists. *Ere Nouvelle,* in an 1848 editorial, maintained that improving the lot of the workers did not have to take place at the cost of ruining others. As Christians believe in the reconciliation of all things, earthly and heavenly, in God, the duty of Christians was to act as mediators between the conflicting classes. Similar ideas were voiced by Lammenais, in Germany by Baader and von Ketteler.

The role of private property was an inevitable subject in a discussion of capitalism. It apparently created no difficulty among those evaluating the Social Question from the Catholic standpoint. They took for granted that property was a gift from God and had to be used in conformity with His will. They admitted no such thing as "absolute" property. It had to be used in a socially responsible way. Von Ketteler wrote in 1848, "In its doctrine on the concept of property the Catholic Church has nothing in common with the idea on property rights that are generally current in

the world, according to which man regards himself as the absolute
master of the things he owns. Never can the Church allow men the right
to deal and traffic with the bounties of this earth guided only by their
whims." If people would use their property in conflict with the laws of
God, public authority was called upon to enforce the social controls
required to make its use accord with Christian principles.[2]

This implication of public authority in private affairs was the general
view of these individuals. The state was an essential participant in producing social change. Ozanam and others warned, people would not be
satisfied with a political revolution alone. There was need also for a
social revolution in which the assistance of the state was essential. It
would have to sponsor social legislation, promote workers' associations,
supervise social reforms.

Indeed, the political revolution was considered the prerequisite for the
more important social revolution. Ozanam's slogan, "Avoid politics and
concentrate on the social question," was widely accepted. Von Ketteler
voiced the same opinion. Von Baader—creator of the concept of Christian Socialism—wrote in 1835 that merely to give the individual political
liberties would not make him free; he also needed "social liberty" to
make him completely free.[3]

When the ideas of these nineteenth century people are taken in their
totality, their early twentieth century counterparts have added little to
an analysis of the causes and cures for poverty.

With the arrival of the twentieth century, the Social Question moved
into the background. The worst results of industrialization were being
overcome. During the first half of the century social legislation was progressing. The problem of poverty was handled by governments and
political parties (including Catholic parties). "Charity," social work,
education, health services, and so on, were undertaken more by secular
than religious institutions and accepted—however inadequately—as routine. Theology could and did devote itself to other social problems. The
appalling condition of the poor in colonial areas and Latin America were
practically ignored by theologians. The lower clergy and missionaries
took care of the poor with customary charity and education.

In France, more than in Germany or other European countries,
Catholicism was preoccupied with its revival on a fairly high, abstract
intellectual level. Catholic political parties and labor unions devoted
themselves to the task of advancing social legislation, succeeding better
in some than in other European countries. But changing social structures
was not in their platforms.

The successors of these nineteenth century Catholic theologians, until
the arrival of the Liberation theologians, were occupied mainly with
creating often highly abstruse and sophisticated variations on theological themes. Many devoted themselves to the practical execution and

application of the principles worked out by their predecessors. They developed an intense activity in establishing new organizations, study and research groups, educational associations, and, most important, political parties. These activities were useful. But they reached relatively small sections of the population, relative, that is, to secular movements of the time—foremost socialism and socialist organizations. These activities were not based on an inspiring social doctrine that could have competed successfully with the appeals of Marxism and, later, other sociopolitical ideologies and activities. The Christian social movement lacked a great theorist who could formulate Christian principles to attract the society at large, it did not lack the principles for the correction of the capitalist abuses. But, one may add, even in the presence of a great theorist, the cautious and incremental ways of the church in adjusting doctrine and Magisterium would have placed a damper on the translation of theory into practice.

When, in the following pages, the thoughts and actions of Liberation theologians are surveyed, one cannot escape the question why the Vatican criticizes them so much for their alleged Marxism when most of their sociological ideas concerning poverty can be found among clergymen and theologians throughout the nineteenth century and in the social encyclicals of the twentieth century. The major and innovative theological contribution of the Liberation theologians appears to be much less objectionable in Rome. The suspicion is difficult to abandon that hostility against the Liberation theologians is largely due to what they are doing rather than what they are saying.

9
The Remedies of the
Liberation Theologians

Liberation theologians have introduced at least two novelties in their suggestion for remedies of poverty. One is assigning to the church and religion a substantial responsibility for material improvements in life on earth as a preparation for entry into the Kingdom of Heaven. This is the consequence of considering poverty not a social category, but a religious concept. The other novelty lies in their encouragement of action to translate principles into reality. This is the consequence of too much rhetoric and not enough action on the part of the official church.

On both counts, the Gospel is the foundation of their position. Their interpretation demands comprehensive religious and secular activity going beyond the traditional range of action by either the church or Catholic Action. Perhaps it would be more correct to say that as a result of their interpretation of the Gospel, what used to be considered secular activities have assumed for them a religious character and a religious legitimization. At the same time, they are asking the church to slant these activities toward the side of the poor, thereby endowing the preferential option for the poor with concrete contents.

These theologians derive their suggestions from two passages in *Gaudium et spes,* 1965 nos. 39, 72. Christians are there admonished to take an active part, in the name of religion, in present-day socio-economic development. They are to fight for justice and charity, while always observing "the right order in their earthly activities in faithfulness to Christ and the Gospel," meaning, presumably, giving spiritual preference to material liberation. The second passage refers to a future kingdom on earth, a kingdom that "is already present in mystery. When the Lord returns it will be brought into full flower." The expectation of this kingdom on earth must "stimulate our concern for cultivating this one."

Most Liberation theologians have no intention of remedying poverty by building the Kingdom of God on earth here and now, nor to interpret it as a political kingdom. They share the belief that all things are redeemed and reconciled in Christ "whether they be things on earth or things in heaven" (Col. 1:2). But people are on earth bodily as subjects making their history through work (Gen. 1:28) and, the theologians argue, charity and love in earthly action are part of the Eucharist. Gutiérrez pointed out that the struggle for a just society is part of salvation history.[1] Improving life on earth for all, but especially the poor, prepares people for entry into the Kingdom of Heaven. "The right order" is thereby maintained and the kingdom on earth "cultivated."

The theologians are asking the church to live up to her demands for social and economic changes. This emphatic request is not tantamount to reducing the Gospel to a purely "earthly gospel," but merely reminding the church to practice what she is preaching. Possible political risks are of no great relevance to them. Most of them find political action desirable and inevitable, as well as a part of salvation history.

The Liberation theologians' concern with the poor raises the question of whom they are including in this category? To them, the poor are the spiritually and materially poor. Leonardo Buff includes the economically poor, the politically deprived, the uneducated, the sick—all of which goes hand in hand in Latin America. Many expand the concept to embrace those who suffer with and for the poor without being poor themselves. The official church, since Constantine and Theodosius, has not taken such a broad view for a long time. Its restriction to alms giving automatically limited the category of the poor, reflecting a paternalistic attitude, ignoring the possibility of self-help by the poor and unduly narrowing the Gospel concept of the spiritually poor.

The *Instruction on Certain Aspects of "Liberation Theology,"* 1984, IX-10, accuses these theologians of "disastrously" confusing the poor of the Scripture with the proletariat of Marx. Quite apart from the fact that the theologians deal more with peasants than industrial workers, many encyclicals speak of the "proletariat" and "proletarization" without having a Marxist character. The poor of Liberation Theology are identical with those of these encyclicals, possibly including more groups than the encyclicals, and certainly more than Marxism, even adjusted Marxism's proletariat. Moreover, the theologians' concern with the poor on earth is an integral part also of the poor's spiritual life on their way to a future life in heaven.

These theologians see no justification in dividing a person's total existence into a now and a future, and then to neglect the first part in favor of the second. This earns them the accusation of contradicting the traditional teaching of the church and of using an unacceptable hermeneutic.

This separation of a person's existence into two parts goes back centuries. Many encyclicals of the nineteenth century and most of more recent date no longer maintain it. But as the accusation shows, the idea has not yet been entirely discarded. Unfortunately, when Marx looked at the society of the early industrial revolution from the standpoint of the proletariat, traditional theology was unhelpful to him. By separating body and soul, and then devoting itself mainly to the welfare of the soul at the neglect of material existence on earth, the Gospel provided no guidance for him.[2]

The theologians think, as do many popes, that the time has come to abolish this shortcoming. They maintain, briefly, in order to justify their activism, that there is no single uniform teaching or hermeneutic in Catholicism any more than there is in Liberation Theology. As Pope John Paul II once said, "Liberation theology, yes, but which one?" The same could be said of various aspects of Catholicism when the changing nature of the Magisterium is considered.

Historical reflection can lead to a variety of theological conclusions without necessarily interfering with the fundamentals of Christian faith. These theologians, in justifying their methods for helping the poor, point to the great differences of Catholicism to be found between the present and the past, between countries, even between regions within one country. After all, the Gospel reflected existing, living conditions. It arose in the context of the social reality of a given society at a given time. If it is to be relevant today, the contemporary environment, history, culture must affect its interpretation at many levels. This fact is evident in the strongly European nature of contemporary Catholicism; the difficulty of reconciling Catholicism with African culture, tradition, and experiences; or even in the reflection of the Polish experience of Pope John Paul II.

In the choice of their remedies the Liberation theologians fully acknowledge—more so than their nineteenth century predecessors, or at least more consciously so—the universally valid ethical principles of Catholicism and the spirit of the Gospel. Both are used as guides to policy and practice, but in the light of the Latin American experience, or perhaps better, in the light of the local experience, considering that the theology can now be found in many parts of the world. Denying the existence of a single exclusively valid hermeneutic, José Croatto wrote, "The theology of the Third World has burst upon the scene with a hermeneutic challenge. Like the theology that is arising in the world of the poor, all theologies of Liberation (socio-political, religious, women's, black, 'theologic,' and so on) mean to decipher a liberating God's new manifestation in situations of injustice and alienation."[3]

The Liberation theologians reject an abstract, monolithic theology equally valid everywhere. Their interpretation of the Gospel and Christology in the light of the Latin American experiences produces remedies of an idiosyncratic nature, not even suitable alike for every Latin

American country. Their common denominator is a stress on earthly remedies and, in line with the warning of the *Instruction on Christian Freedom and Liberation,* 1986, a stress also on the contribution of economics to spiritual liberation.

The remedies proposed by these theologians range from theologically conservative but sociologically progressive (e.g. José Comblin) to a comprehensive radicalism (e.g. Hugo Assmann, José Miranda), yet all based upon Catholicism (as they understand it, of course). They also have in common that they are suspect (to say the least) in important circles of the Vatican and to many clergy in high and low positions in many parts of the world.

Charity and love, or charity as love, is as central to Liberation Theology as it is to all other theologies. Gutiérrez, Boff and others have emphasized that to be saved means to reach the fullness of love, and that faith is salvific only when it is translated into praxis of love. This basic condition distinguishes Liberation Theology at once from Marxism, the ethic of which is based on class struggle, tolerating neither (Christian) faith nor salvation into another world.

Charity is not considered equal to alms giving. Alms giving is described as inadequate because it does not cover many aspects of poverty, because it is provided on an individual basis and does not touch the social root of the evil. What is needed, the theologians say, is social charity: charity referring to a person in the economic, social, cultural, racial environment. Charity means being everybody's neighbor, especially the neighbor of the poor, and includes material as well as spiritual concerns. It means, above all, action, going out to meet a person and being a neighbor. "Faith without works is dead" (James 2:20). Finally, faith means permeating all human relations with the spirit of love. This interpretation of charity and love, say the theologians, contrary to the implication of the *Instruction on Christian Freedom and Liberation,* 1986, does not restrict the theology to the class of the poor. It encompasses all human beings.

When so interpreted, charity cannot be accomplished by conversion alone, certainly not when it is restricted to alms giving. Catholics and their church are committed to more comprehensive action. This broader kind of charity requires a committed love that translates into the preferential option for the poor. Reaching this goal requires action to eliminate the broadly conceived poverty and this, in turn, requires changes in the society. Popes and Boff have pointed out that societies are in situations of structural and social (i.e. collective) sin. Social change therefore becomes part of conversion derived directly from the Gospel.

What changes the Liberation theologians require emerges from their socio-historical analysis of contemporary society, or better, their Latin American contemporary society. They find it characterized by a class structure causing poverty. This objective condition must be judged in the light of the faith, with the criteria of judgment supplied by a theological and ethical order. Action must follow. At that time, the church must sublimate the features of liberation in its practice, doctrine, Magisterium, theology, and apply them. In accordance with these features, the church must mobilize the society and its people. The poor, in particular, need to be mobilized because an oppressive society has immobilized them too long. This is the mobilization taking place in the Ecclesiastic Base Communities, now scattered across Latin America and many other parts of the globe. There, a social conscience is formed; self-responsibility and self-improvement are discovered. A desire for change is the consequence and an awareness of the possibility of bringing it about is awakened. In cooperation with all classes sympathetic to the cause of the poor, so the theologians are hoping, total liberation can be achieved.

Liberation theologians agree with other theologians and some popes that the politico-economic system of Latin America is primarily responsible for the poverty of the masses and the spiritual poverty of the rich. When the bishops at Puebla in 1979 concluded that poverty was not a passing stage but the product of definite economic, social, and political situations and structures, making the rich richer and the poor poorer,[4] they merely confirmed *Populorum progressio,* 1967, and anticipated *Laborem exercens,* 1981. Even the *Instruction,* 1984, conceded the need for structural changes as a subsidiary measure. But this concession failed to satisfy some Liberation theologians (e.g. Juan Segundo) because the document did not draw the consequences of its own conclusion. It only aimed at individuals, advocating, again, personal conversion. It ignored the existence of social sin located in the social structures, though this was already foreshadowed in *Quadragesiomo anno* in 1931.

In the view of the theologians, this is not an either/or proposition. Conversion and social change are both needed to make liberation complete. Nor do the theologians agree with the greatly differing emphasis the *Instruction,* 1984, placed on material and spiritual liberation. They recognize spiritual liberation as the major goal, with, however, material liberation as its indispensable prerequisite.

The views of the Liberation theologians on private property are determined by the role it plays in sustaining those aspects of the system they believe need change. Very few not very prominent theologians favor the abolition of private property altogether. Most subscribe to the proposition of the late encyclicals that private property must be used in a socially responsible way and that there is a social mortgage on it. Gutiérrez agreed expressly with Pope John Paul II that "certain" means of production may have to be socialized and that the accumulation of "excessive" wealth is un-Christian. He and some others would presumably go further toward socialism, without, however, subscribing to any orthodox form of Marxism and certainly not to any existing form. Their strong commitment to the Gospel would prevent them from doing so. (But whether this statement can be maintained in regard to Leonardo Boff, who showed great enthusiasm for the Soviet system after his visit to the Soviet Union in 1987, is questionable.)

On the class struggle, the Liberation theologians agree with the present position of the official church that it is not ordained by God. But they have not shown any enthusiasm for the solution of Pope John Paul II that if all classes were to cooperate toward solidarity, the problem of class conflict could be solved. For them, the question remains acute regarding how the unity, universality, and community of the church and the faithful could be achieved and social inequalities could disappear in a system with the built-in feature of class conflict?

Liberation theologians believe that the church must join with the poor to elevate their status, since it is they, not the rich, who need help. To be neutral in the class struggle, said Gutiérrez many times, is impossible.[5] It would in effect mean siding with the powerful, who maintain the unjust system. Virtually no theologian recommends class warfare as a method of choice. There are, however, considerable differences in what they do advocate, ranging from passive resistance to violent revolution, depending upon what a given situation requires. Participation in class struggle has been commonplace in Latin America ever since independence and the lower clergy led the masses in their struggle for social justice.[6] There prevails, at any rate, a considerable skepticism about the conversion of capitalists in Latin America, the more so as capitalism in Latin America is today firmly embedded in an international system entirely beyond the reach of the poor.

This broadening base of capitalism across the globe and its internationalization have enhanced a nationalism that had already played a role in the growth of Liberation Theology from its beginnings. Under its impact, as has been pointed out, class conflict is seen no longer limited to classes within countries. It has been transferred to dominant versus dominated countries. Many theologians (including Pope John Paul II) agree that the "internal" colonizers have joined with major American and other foreign interests in support of exploitive, oppressive systems in Latin America. For many theologians, liberation now includes national political liberation from colonialist insiders and outsiders and associates them with Dependency theory.

This expansion of course antagonizes foreign capitalists. It also worries the official church in Rome for political reasons. For it will affect the foreign policies of Latin American countries, as well as policies of foreign countries toward Latin America, with the church having to maneuver carefully in a very complex situation. The theologians take the' caution of Rome as another indication of the church's Euro-centrism and its inability to understand Latin American conditions—and therefore to appreciate the remedies proposed by the Liberation theologians.

The opposition to imperialism by the Liberation theologians has been taken as evidence of their Marxism. Yet, in the first place, their opposition to foreign control was most likely generated by Latin America's historical experience, not Marxism. In the second place, a number of recent encyclicals were severely condemning various forms of imperialism. In the third place, at the end of the twentieth century, opposition to imperialism can hardly be considered a Marxist monopoly anymore. There may be indicators of Marxism among Liberation theologians; anti-imperialism is not one of them.

Actually, socialist principles as remedies for poverty have found a mixed reception among Liberation theologians. Few generalizations are possible. Socialism is, in any case, not a necessary part of the theology. Some theologians fear socialist principles, some oppose them. Most accept modified forms of socialism. Yet others pick and choose from socialism, like their predecessors in the nineteenth century. Many borrow Marxist methods of analysis. But whatever they select, no theologian fails to integrate the choice with Catholicism. Popes have not been averse to such eclectic methods regarding socialism by express references to it.

Quadragesimo anno, 1931 no. 116, had cautiously suggested that "socialist claims, so far as they are just" are better taken care of by Christian faith and charity. Pope Paul VI in his letter *Octogesima adveniens,* 1971, differentiated between various levels in the expression of socialism: "a generous aspiration and a seeking of a more just society, historical movements with a political organization and aim, and an ideology which claims to give a complete and self-sufficient picture of man." Pope John XXIII envisaged cooperation with Communists for certain purposes.[7]

The contemporary Vatican (or members of its officialdom) rejects these efforts at selectivity. It considers Marxism a complete, integrated system, predetermining all social analysis and data as derived from the fundamental ideology. Accepting any part of it would inevitably lead to accepting all of it. This attitude is detailed in the *Instruction* of 1984 and represents a regression to pre-1931 times.

Liberation theologians deny the Vatican's argumentation. Most readily admit in any case that socialism is far from solving all earthly social problems; that at best it could only represent part of the comprehensive liberation they are aiming at. Even John O'Donohue, an opponent of Liberation Theology, wrote, "If the word 'socialism' is used to denote a practical program for freeing human beings from unnecessary obstacles to their authentic development, then every decent human being must be a socialist, and therefore every Christian."[8]

There is no reason to assume that most theologians or encyclicals accept the concept of socialism or parts of it in any other sense, and only so much of it as conforms with this sense. This possibility exists, contrary to the assumption of the *Instruction*, 1984, because socialism is not monolithic, either in theory or practice. Besides, coincidences between aspects of a great variety of ideologies must be taken for granted when they deal with such complex and enormous topics as human beings and their societies.

One of the attractions of whatever socialist principles Liberation theologians adopt is socialism's seemingly correct analysis of the contemporary Latin American condition. For, more than any other social analysis, it clarifies the conditions underlying the alienation and exploitation of the poor masses. It leads to the conclusion, accepted by the theologians, that the members of the Latin American (or any other) dominating class are poor subjects for conversion from sin. The theologians do, of course, not reject the idea of conversion from sin. But they expect the process to be a very long one. In the meantime they want to exploit all available temporal means to help the poor. But they have little guidance to do this innovatively in conformity with their religious beliefs because, as Edward Schillebeeckx once remarked "The evangelical message gives us no direct program of social political action."

The nineteenth century theologians struggled with the same problem. They too called for social change without knowing what change was required or how it could be brought about. Meanwhile they had recourse to the more traditional ways of the church to relieve poverty. Later, socialism, and following it chronologically and rhetorically, several encyclicals had suggestions for the replacement of sinful structures resembling socialist principles, without providing guidance for their implementation. Their application would have required an undisguised involvement in politics and economics, always an odious matter for the church. The "running" of politics and economics is not a "direct part of the Church's mission in society" said the *Instruction* of 1986 no. 61. This posture would excuse the church from supporting Liberation theologians should they become involved in such "running."

But this posture also creates a problem. How could the inevitably political fight against poverty and structural sin be conducted if the church chooses to stay out of politics and if at the same time oligarchies stubbornly uphold that structure, occasionally with the support of the clergy to boot? If the Vatican were serious about abolishing "sinful structures" and "evil mechanisms," it could use weapons so far not used (excommunication, etc.). Much to the chagrin of some circles in the Vatican, however, the Liberation theologians are helping to develop means for the masses to hasten their own liberation. These means are the Ecclesiastic Base Communities and the People's Church.

During the last two decades or so, there have arisen in Latin America and thereafter elsewhere Ecclesiastic Base Communities—in other words, grass roots communities, Communidades Ecclesiales de Base— and a People's Church, or Iglesia Popular. The communities were started in Panama in 1963 by missionaries from Chicago. There are some 150,000 in Brazil, fewer in other countries, and a very few can even be found in Canada and Switzerland. The aim of these institutions is to generate comprehensive, urgently needed, and innovative changes, not only where they are established but also as precedents for imitation in localities across the globe. The communities consider themselves a part of the church and are operated by religious or laypersons, due to the shortage of priests.

The Ecclesiastical Base Communities appear in a great variety of forms. Common features are regular meetings of the members as Christians, worshipping together, trying to understand their situation in the light of the Gospel, and then using their knowledge to improve their situation in and through the community; to gain self-understanding as God's people; to learn democratic methods as a step toward their liberation; to develop nonviolent methods in application of their newly discovered political power; to train laypersons—men and women—for leadership roles, including religious leadership.

The communities are self-reliant. They help members to realize and develop their individual identities. Contacts are established locally and regionally among people who have previously had no knowledge of each other and their similar problems. Using their Christianity as legitimization, and within local limits and resources, they provide for education, health, shelter, clothing, nourishment, and generally for the improvement of their villages or urban slums. The communities have helped to replace fatalism with hope, and, so many observers report, perhaps for the first time have made Christianity real and meaningful to their members.

Underlying these communities is the Liberation theologians' conviction that the poor must play the major role in raising their own status. This is the aim of "conscientization" (Paolo Freire), enabling the poor to discover the social causes of their misery and their right and the possibility of doing something about it. Through this method the demeaning implications of receiving alms is eliminated, while at the same time the poor are made aware of their power. The method is in accord with the *Quadragesimo anno*, 1931 no. 141, admonition that "the first and immediate apostles to the workers should be the workers; the apostles to those who follow industry and trade ought to be from among themselves."

Leonardo Boff hailed the arrival of the communities as "one of the great principles of church renewal worldwide."[9] The final document of the Puebla Conference called them a cause for "joy and hope in the Church" and affirmed that their vitality "is now beginning to bear fruit."[10] In the process of evangelization, the document continues, "the validity of the experience embodied in the EBCs will be recognized, and their further growth in communion with their pastors will be fostered," provided they will not fall prey to outside influences and remain faithful to the church. Pope John Paul II, Leonardo Boff announced in 1980, had written a wonderful letter about the Base Communities. Further, according to Boff (in his book *Ecclesiogenesis* and elsewhere), the communities reflect the spirit of Christianity by the absence of alienating structures, by direct relationships, by mutualities and deep communion, by common Gospel studies and by equality among all members.

Charging the poor masses of Latin America with being the protagonists of their own liberation (Gutiérrez) is placing a heavy burden upon them. For centuries they have been marginalized. The means of even being aware of their lowly position, let alone of being able to do something about it, had been withheld from them. The bishops at Medellín, 1968, affirmed that it was their duty now to satisfy the urgent need for conscientizing evangelization which would inspire and direct all the initiatives toward the formation of the people in the poor villages and slums. A foremost task would be to restore their human dignity after it had been destroyed for centuries.

The people in the communities, together with the supporting Liberation theologians, though focussing their activities upon their localities, have nevertheless to overcome political adversities. They now have to contend with the suspicions and disapproval of Catholic authorities on ecclesiastical grounds, and with the harassment from worldly authorities on political grounds, with both often joining to defend their respective interests. It must be taken for granted that Marxists and Communists will attempt to infiltrate the communities. And also that Marxists will affect efforts to improve the members' social situation. However, the Gospel is the guide for the liberation and, indeed, all activities in the communities. There is no attempt to replace Christianity with Marxist ideology, or liberation through faith with violent revolution. The guns some members carry in the fields are for defense against outsiders, not for violent upheavals.

In spite of numerous encyclicals advocating political education of the faithful as important, raising the political consciousness of the poor has been opposed. The church fears too much emphasis upon worldly matters, the growth of a second or a class church, a parallel magisterium. The ruling elites fear a threat to their dominant positions.

The theologians remain undeterred by the resistance. They assert that nothing incompatible with the Gospel occurs in the communities. The fear that the church or religion become politicized is rejected as unrealistic because the church is now and always has been deeply involved in politics. Gutiérrez pointed out that the Gospel message of total love "has an inescapable political dimension" when it is addressed to people living in subhuman conditions.[11] The Liberation theologians resent being singled out by the official church on this ground when many bishop conferences in other countries publish extensive and relatively radical statements on economics, human rights, and other politically sensitive topics without being reprimanded by Rome.

Obviously, this particular method of politicizing the poor can succeed only to the degree that Latin American states become democratized. The political opposition uses every means to prevent this from happening. Nevertheless, the communities are slowly progressing. They have become an integral part of their members' lives and have improved their material and spiritual existence. Most observers are very favorably impressed. Attempts to suppress them, together with Liberation Theology, seem no longer possible. Hans Küng remarked that it was too late for the Vatican to silence the theologians "because they have already been heard and understood by millions of Christians."[12] Nevertheless the efficacy of the communities appears to depend largely on their leadership, often supplied by the local church. Where bishops are favorable to Liberation Theology, the success of the communities is likely to be greater than in localities where bishop and clergy are not particularly favorable.

What the long-run effect of the activities of Liberation theologians will be remains to be seen. Neither they nor the official church have outlined in detail a future political or social system fitting the projected "civilization of love." In the meantime, however, the members of the Ecclesiastic Base Communities have been uplifted religiously, morally, economically, and socially. The result outdistances any other achieved by enterprises of the past trying to reach the same goal.

The picture of the People's church is less clear. The dividing lines between the Base Communities, religious activities, and the official church are difficult to draw. Adding to the confusion is the existence of a popular religion ("el popular"), that is, the people's version of Catholicism. This popular religion is a composite of elements from orthodox Catholicism, folkloristic beliefs preceding the introduction of Catholicism, and idiosyncratic biblical interpretations arising spontaneously from the experience of people in the communities.[13] It dates back to the arrival of Christianity, which gave Latin American society "a confused, perplexing mysticism that was the essence of the fusion of two civilizations."[14]

The popular religion does not break links with the official church. It is now beginning to act as a ferment within it, leading to mutual influence and adjustments. The somewhat unorthodox religious practices in the communities are due largely to the failure of the official church to make its teaching relevant to the poor masses. They are also due to the shortage of priests, especially native priests. The question has therefore been raised whether men and women with experience in the communities may not be ordained as priests on a part-time basis. After all, the argument is, the church exists to serve the community, not the other way around.

The official church has criticized some communities as being too politicized and too preoccupied with material existence. It has been most anxious about the growth of a formal People's church parallel to the official church, as a threat to the unity of the Catholic church. These fears may not be unfounded if Rome responds to Latin American religious developments with rejection rather than adaptation. Such adaptation would require less opposition to material concerns, more opposition to the forces oppressing the poor, and a more prominent presence of the church in the countryside. Otherwise, conscientization might indeed lead to the growth of a new church "from below."

There have been persistent denials that a People's church in any organized, institutionalized form exists. Yet, Bishop Oscar Romero, shortly before he was murdered, created the National Conference of the People's Church (CONIP) in El Salvador in 1980. At the same time some groups appeared among Nicaragua's clergy, including some bishops, forming loosely organized communities resembling a People's church. In other countries, some bishops encouraged the creation of independent religious communities. In yet others, bishops strengthened links between the Base Communities and the official church either to control the communities (e.g. in Colombia) or to establish better relations with the poor (e.g. in Brazil).

The existence of the Ecclesiastical Base Communities and the People's church poses a challenge to the official church and some governments. There is an unavoidable connection between the Theology of Liberation, the communities and the People's church or popular religion on the one hand, and the social mobilization and progressive activities of the masses in villages and slums on the other. The growing political awareness, the self-reliant liberation activity, and the rise of leaders from the communities creating new organizations for the poor are novel phenomena in Latin America. They show that rhetoric (e.g. in many encyclicals) can have consequences among those toward whom it is directed that were unexpected by those who voiced it.

The Base Communities, where they function freely, very likely contribute a share to trends in some Latin American states toward a weakening of dictatorships, possibly even toward democratization and social justice. In some states (e.g. Brazil) this process appeared so pronounced that pressure from CELAM and the Vatican was applied to slow it down, mainly with a view to depoliticize it. Yet, once again, Pope John Paul II during his travels in Latin America in May 1988, warned the big landowners of the "social mortgage" on their property, even while he warned Peruvian bishops that aspects of Liberation Theology, especially class warfare, were unwelcome to the church. His heart, he said, was close to those dedicated to union activity, since unions were a just vehicle to achieve social harmony.[15] Members of the Base Communities could interpret these words as encouragement of their activities (as, presumably, could the Polish workers on strike at that time).

The Liberation theologians, as the providers of the religious legitimization of these activities and sometimes the participants, bear the brunt of criticism emanating from the opponents of the Theology and its practical consequences. The violence of opposition from secular and religious sources may be an index of the success the Theology is having in showing a way for remedying the fate of the poor in Latin America and, indeed, beyond.

10
Violence as a Remedy for Poverty

Revolution is a concept the official church uses to describe rapid, radical, but nonviolent social changes. It has been tolerant of (just!) wars between states but not individual groups. "Revolutionary force is a priori suspect," wrote Walter Dirks.[1]

When Pope Paul VI was in Latin America in 1968, he declared the use of force to be neither Christian nor evangelical. Violent changes of social structures, he warned, are deceiving and inefficient, as well as incompatible with the dignity of the people. He added in his Apostolic Exhortation *Evangelii nuntiandi*, 1975 no. 36, that the most ideal structures become inhuman if the people living in them fail to convert heart and mind. Thereafter, the Latin American episcopate confirmed that neither maintaining the security of the state by means of terror nor the spreading of messianism by the guerrillas through brutalities conform to the spirit of the Evangelium.

This stance is not rigid. The church would not actively instigate a violent revolution. But it might tolerate others engaging in it, as it has in the past tolerated violence by groups with which it was associated.

Pope Paul VI, though decrying the use of force, sanctioned a "revolutionary uprising" in *Populorum progressio*, 1967 no. 31, on condition that "there is manifest, long-standing tyranny which would do great damage to fundamental personal rights and dangerous harm to the common good of the country." *The Instruction of Christian Freedom and Liberation*, 1986 no. 79, reconfirmed that the Magisterium admits "as a last resort" recourse to armed struggle against an oppressive tyranny.

But revolution is forbidden "to make far-reaching reforms and to suppress unjustifiable privileges." The extremely limited authorization of the Magisterium to use force is hedged in with so many qualifications, no situation is likely to arise in which the use of force might be permitted. Nevertheless, there is a slight breach in the dam the church has erected against violence.

A widening of the breach is conceivable. The church has already pinpointed social structures in Latin American countries contributing to tyranny and producing poverty and inequality. According to the testimony of several popes, conversion has failed to arrest a deterioration of the situation. Greater pressure for reforms has been paralleled by more ruthless oppression and exploitation of the poor masses. As the church has adopted the idea of integral liberation, efforts must therefore begin on earth to realize eschatological promises. But, as Carl E. Braaten has written, "The attempt to seek every possible approximation of . . . eschatologial hopes already in this life, in this world, will inevitably create revolutionary situations."[2] In the environment of Latin America and some other Third World countries, such situations would likely be exploited and exploded by secular ideologues and leaders, as well as by some theologians who believe that for one or another significant reason, violence may have to be the price of liberty.

There are a few theologians who have already decided that violent revolution alone can bring about the desired social changes. These are mostly the theologians struggling to synthesize Christianity and Marxism (but who should not be confused with those numerous theologians using or seemingly using Marxism instrumentally for social analysis). At the other extreme are those few who are pacifists and would not sanction the use of violence under any circumstances. Between the two extremes are the great number of theologians hoping to create a better world or bringing about social change peacefully. But they envisage and usually accept the possibility that the peaceful process might turn into a violent one when the rich and powerful would resist social change diminishing their privileges.

This scenario is more likely to be found in the Third World than in the First World, where sinful structures are rigid and unfavorable to the marginalized poor. For that reason, some Liberation theologians find the Political Theology of their First World fellow theologians not transferable to the Third World. The politics sustaining and resisting extreme politics always contain the seeds of violence.

Whether violence will break out, at what point, and with what intensity would depend upon the nature of the theology being applied and would, in any case, be unpredictable with any accuracy. But virtually all Liberation theologians are prophylactically providing some justification for possible violence in their scheme: To the extent that they are tolerating violence, it would be counterviolence against the violence of the oppressors of the poor. Such violence by the poor could be sanctioned as self-defense or in the manner the church permits "just war."

Leonardo Boff typically asserted that the poor as Christians would resort to violence only if their oppressors would force them to do so. Similarly, José Comblin opposed the use of violence. But if a person confronted with the choice between liberating action, which might lead to violence or no action, which would permit oppression to continue, the first course must be chosen.

The joint Ecumenical Council of Churches and the papal commission Justitia et Pax, after meeting in 1971, called on the churches to examine to what extent violent social structures could be changed by the potentially risky employment of the church's political and economic power to make them more serviceable to the causes of freedom and justice and peace. Christians living in a violent environment may want to opt for bringing about law and order or a change by nonviolent action. In the final conclusions, the meeting of these groups could go no further because of the threefold division of opinion of the pacifists, the radicals willing to use violence after the exhaustion of other means, and those who were already living in a situation dominated by violence that gave them no choice but to use counterviolence. They agreed, however, as in the admonition of the *Instruction,* 1986, that before violence was used, the situation had to be thoroughly examined and a "positive" conception of the future order had to be developed. Only in this case could the use of violence be considered an "act of freedom" and count on God's forgiveness.[3] Other theologians (e.g. Jürgen Moltmann) similarly saw the use of violence legitimized only by the humane aims of a violent revolution.

The last point refers to a vexing problem. How could anyone be certain a peaceful world would emerge from the use of violence, which is the only legitimate use of violence? Violence begets violence, and many wars have been fought to end all wars. It must be forever doubtful whether the brotherhood of man would indeed arise if the poor stopped being poor and social justice would prevail. Those theologians willing to take a chance on violence are hardly dealing with this problem. They rationalize that rescuing the poor would be the use of "good violence," as distinguished from the "bad violence" of the oppressors. The French Marxist Roger Garaudy gave them the answer when he wrote that humans never have a choice between violence and no violence, but only between two kinds of violence, with everybody having to decide for himself in each case which kind will allow a greater freedom to develop.

In the final analysis the Gospel and the Magisterium supply no definitive solution to the problem of creating a just social order or undoing an unjust one. The writings of many theologians give the impression that while tolerating violence, if necessary, they feel nevertheless uneasy about their tolerance.

The existence of a "positive conception" of the future order as a prerequisite for the legitimate use of violence can hardly ever be fulfilled. First, how "positive" is positive? Second, the decision among the parties to use violence would probably evaporate before they could reach agreement on the details of a future social order. In practice, violence under the conditions established by the church and many Liberation theologians is a nonexisting option – which is probably the result the church wants to achieve.

PART II
The Politics of Poverty

The problem of poverty has assumed a new urgency since the middle of the twentieth century. The reasons were the emergence of the Third World with its masses of poor people, the worldwide preoccupation with human rights and, perhaps, the bad conscience of the wealthier classes. In the First World the problem remains far from solved but does not have the acuteness or preeminence it possesses in the Third World. The lessons the Catholic church had learned during the last almost two hundred years in dealing with poverty should enable it to handle the problem in a more efficient way now than in the past. This is all the more true as the situation in Latin America in particular has remarkable parallels with that of nineteenth century Europe, which is one of the reasons why the book now concentrates on Latin America. One helpful difference from the past is the recognition by the church that poverty is also the result of "sinful structures" as well as sinful people. Its occasional apparent willingness to apply this knowledge to the solution of the poverty problem in Latin America, will deeply involve it in Latin American politics. For now the church must challenge in addition to individual sinners, the system favored by an entire benefitting class with which, moreover, it was, and in some cases still is, in collusion.

Church involvement in politics is nothing new. The only question has always been where on the political spectrum it would stand, which side it would support. Its position would depend sometimes on internal church, sometimes on external conditions. Reactions to the politics of the church by governments and other secular forces varied accordingly. But, in any case, the church has learned that the instrumental use of religion for other than spiritual ends is usually hazardous and has made it cautious.

For some 170 years after the eighteenth century revolutions and the Napoleonic wars, the church was occupied largely with overcoming the extensive damage it had suffered in the turmoil accompanying and following these events. From its efforts emerged a church highly centralized, rigidly hierarchical, insisting on "law and order" within the institution and ideologically conservative. This happened at a time when revolutionary changes in ideologies, science and technology, political and social systems, and ways of life took place in the Western world.

The church had great difficulty participating in this modernization. It tended to ascribe the loss of power and prestige to these new developments and was pining for the good old days. In this mood it became generally critical of innovations but was unable to affect them significantly. Its opposition merely isolated the church even more from the mainstream of the cultural changes characterizing the nineteenth century. It could all too often be found in the forefront of every backward movement. It tied itself to moribund governments, classes, and traditions. It became culturally irrelevant. And the decline of religiosity of the European peoples from at least the middle of last to the middle of this century evidenced the irrelevance of the church also to religion. This (relative) insignificance occurred at a moment when new ideologies and new politics and new economics proved inspiring and exciting to large sectors of the European population.

The conservative attitude of the church in an age of progressivism created an abundance of conflicts between church and state. They usually concerned the relations between them, limited to matters of special concern to the church. The issues were therefore of a relatively specific nature. In free countries the issues related to matters of public policy, such as public versus private education, taxation of churches, marriage, and divorce legislation. In less free and, later, totalitarian countries, they related to the form and volume in which religious activities were tolerated, or to the extent the state could exercise direct control over the church. Occasionally, the church would object to the immorality of particular state policies. Criticism of a regime or an entire system would occur normally only if the very existence of the church in the given country would be threatened.

On the side of the church, conflict was virtually never carried out by action—with extremely rare exceptions, such as a boycott of national politics by the Catholic citizenry of Italy (*non expedit*). It did not directly threaten the fundamentals of any system or, a fortiori, any ruling class. It never participated actively in changing entire political, economic, or social systems, though it may have favored openly and cautiously one or the other system. The principle of the church's position has been expressed by popes many times. The precepts of nature and the Gospel are above human vicissitudes and should therefore not depend upon any particular form of civil government. In conformity with this general principle, Cardinal Gasparri wrote that Pope Pius X nowhere suggested "that the defense of religion should be conducted on ground other than that of existing institutions";[1] an attitude typical of the church for most of the last two hundred years.

The fate of the poor virtually never caused serious conflicts between church and state. There was no reason. The church took care of their suffering by giving alms. Nobody was threatened and the gifts helped moderate whatever rebellious dissatisfactions the poor may have harbored. This situation began to alter when the church accepted the conclusion that a major cause of poverty was the "sinful structure" of society needing change. This was still merely a verbal threat to the ruling class, but a threat nevertheless. Dealing with the poor became a major political issue only when the threat was transposed from words into deeds through the rise of Political Theology in Europe and Ecclesiastical Base Communities first in Latin America and then elsewhere. The statement of Dom Hélder Câmara described the situation: "When I help get food for the poor, and clothing for the poor and housing for the poor, they call me a saint. When I ask why the people are poor, they call me a Marxist." Or Gutiérrez: "Giving food and drink has in our days become a political act."[2]

In Latin America, for a long time and until the middle of the twentieth century, the official church maintained essentially the same stance that was typical of its earlier stance in Europe. Opposition to independence from Spain and Portugal produced close ties, once again, with the "wrong" side. Eventually, the higher clergy became in Latin America, too, a part of the ruling classes, with the possible difference that they were slightly more concerned with social issues than the European church. But this concern did not amount to identification with any movements for social progress. Nor did it end the official church preoccupation with being and remaining a powerful separate economic entity in an economic system most unfavorable to the poor.

Because Catholicism had considerable influence in Latin America and the church had no serious competition, its role in politics was greater. Governments sought its support for the religious legitimization of their rule. However, this did not prevent endemic struggles between church and state when ideas of the Enlightenment and modern progress got a foothold in Latin America and a small middle class arose at the beginning of this century. Anticlericalism became strong. An anti-Rome feeling also developed with growing nationalism. The political power of the church was reduced, but never eliminated—as was demonstrated, for instance, when the church contributed to the fall of a number of dictators in various countries of Latin America in the middle of the twentieth century. What the church did not succeed in doing, and the ruling classes had little interest in doing, was to integrate the poor masses on the land and in the urban slums into the newer, modernizing societies.

The reasons for this failure, as far as the church is concerned, are well known. The Latin American church is parsimonious and the continent is vast. Available means make it easier to service the cities than the countryside. Priests are scarce (but vocations are improving) and often foreigners because they have to be recruited abroad; some villages do not see one more than once or twice a year. The church was not greatly concerned about the rural masses. It took their religiosity for granted. Catholicism appeared secure. The mostly ceremonial and ritual parts of the Catholic religion, and not what the church considered to be total Catholicism, were integral parts of the peasant's daily life.

A misjudgment of the official church was the powerful hold popular religion had over the masses in Latin America. As was mentioned earlier, by this popular religion ("el popular") is meant a people's religion coexisting with the official church and its hierarchy, theology, and Magisterium in a syncretistic form combining pre-Columbian with Catholic religion. It is a Catholic religion mixed with "superstitious" traditions. Symbols, saints, rites, and rituals have a personal meaning. They are appealed to, as used to be the pagan gods, in concrete situations to provide, miraculously, help and assistance in situations of personal need. The perpetuation of this popular religion is provided by family bonds and a sense of (local) community more than by the priests of a highly structured and institutionalized church. The Ecclesiastic Base Communities reflect this relationship. They represent a challenge to the official church, not a denial of the Catholic religion.[3]

A consequence of "el popular" has been the coexistence, even the combination of, anticlericalism, socialism, communism, or revolution with the popular church and formal Catholicism. The situation was different from the European, where to the official church Catholicism and leftism have been incompatible. The Latin American poor have no difficulty combining both. Liberation theologians refer to this situation when they complain about the lack of understanding of a "Europeanized" official church, or when the Vatican is attempting to force these theologians into making a choice between two opposites where in their mind there is no dichotomy.

In the minds of the Latin American masses—as expressed in "el popular"—relating social issues, that is, their personal needs, to religion is nothing new. When they read the Bible or engage in religious rituals in the context of their daily lives and experiences, they merely find confirmed what they have always believed, namely that they will obtain personal and communal aid from their religious exercises. Thus, while Liberation or any other theology may be highly sophisticated, its translation into daily application and practice is for the masses a down-to-earth matter. Religion for them is a highly personal affair.

Whereas the rise of the welfare state in Europe and the United States was essentially a secular matter, in Latin America, and especially for the Liberation theologians, there is no need for secularizing values in order to promote social welfare. On the contrary, in the presence of popular religion, religion has a considerable influence and is the legitimization of changes in the political, economic, and social conditions. In their own eyes, these theologians, far from being the "social workers" the Vatican is accusing them of being, are working for a Catholic religion that not only justifies but demands these changes. Their difficulty does not lie in the relation between religion and social welfare. It lies in the manner in which the Latin American poor relate religion to their welfare. The popular religion, by making its believers rely upon appeals to saints for miraculous aid or the performance of rites to generate help, tends to make them fatalistic and passive. Help is expected from above, not from one's own efforts. Conscientization has as one of its goals to overcome this surrender to an inevitable fate, by making people realize the human cause of their misery and, hence, be aware of the possibility of doing something about it.

The increasing identification of the official church with social and land reforms in Latin America, a growing independence of the church from the state and its ruling oligarchies, a more successful integration of popular religion into official Catholicism, and a more pronounced sympathy with the social movements flowing through Latin America have made the church less selfish and more important politically. While it might be difficult to find among the clergy individuals opposing the general trend toward a social improvement of the poor masses, considerable conflict and diversity has, however, developed within and without the church over the nature and pace of reforms and who is to control them. It has, in particular, revived the old conflict within the clergy over the nature of relations between church and state. Where the progressives used to criticize the conservatives for their cooperation with reactionary governments, the conservatives are now accusing the leftist clergy for their "interventionism" and for obscuring the line separating the church from the state.

The complex of Liberation Theology with its stress on action has been mainly responsible for the conflict moving into the political arena. It is one thing, obviously, to give alms to the poor or even to appeal to the rich to share their wealth with the poor, and quite another to teach them to act for the improvement of their situation. This is a new approach affecting the politics of the local churches, their relations with their state, their relations with pope and Vatican, and even the international relations of Latin American states.

The politicization of Liberation Theology and the Base Communities in the Latin American context was not surprising. Governments tend to attack the Theology because the political and social mobilization of the poor threatens the power of the ruling classes. The churches are worried and split partly on theological grounds but now also on secular political grounds. Mobilization of the poor masses and sanctioning popular religion might endanger the hierarchical structure of the church and its central control.[4] Where the cooperation between the oligarchy and, especially, the upper echelons of the clergy was still fairly intact, any threat to the oligarchy was considered a threat to the church. Where, as for instance in Nicaragua, the government already considered itself a representative of the masses, the friction developed, on the one hand, between the higher clergy and the government, and, on the other hand, between this section of the clergy and the adherents of Liberation Theology.

The clergy, of course, put their opposition to the Theology in religious terms: The Theology was contrary to the teaching of the church. They shared the fear with the more conservative forces in the Vatican of the rise of a "parallel" church through the Base Communities. And they shared with national governments the fear that the communities might not be religious (in the traditional sense) at all but revolutionary, political, socialist organizations.[5]

The result of these complex political divisions and factionalisms in many Latin American and, particularly, Central American countries, has been the formation of informal and constantly shifting coalitions, most often directed against Liberation Theology and the communities, and varying from country to country.

The motivations of the clergy opposing Liberation Theology has at times been very difficult to discover: whether their cooperation with governments was expedient or whether it was a deliberate identification with the aims of the government. One certainty has been that all parties to the conflicts requested and received outside financial support from many quarters—evidence of the continuing interest and interference of outsiders in the political and religious developments of Latin America.

A most important point to remember is that these high level politics or the sophisticated discussion of this or that theology, and the *Instructions* emanating from the Vatican have relatively little meaning for the priests, nuns, and religious working hard and enthusiastically in the Ecclesiastic Base Communities, the slums, the countryside. In their environment, the Bible has assumed a new, realistic, and practical meaning. Often, they will readily confess that they are not theologians, but religious practitioners intent upon helping the poor out of their incredible misery and the clutches of their exploiters.

Generalizations on the Base Communities are difficult because they appear, even within the same country, in a very great variety. But what can be said with almost general validity is that in practice they are credited by secular and religious authorities with greater significance for church and secular politics than their influence seems to warrant. Their rejection or support by higher religious or worldly institutions depend upon local conditions. Their activities become politicized not because the members are politicians but because in many places the secular oligarchy fears the political consequences of "conscientizing" the poor and is using every means to keep them in their low status. The official church hierarchy is often worried about them lest loss of control over them may threaten the unity of the church or good relations with governments.

Theology, some of the religious workers say, is a luxury they do not have time to afford. In general, some governments have more reason for concern than the church hierarchy. The focus of the thoughts and actions of community workers and members is on relieving the misery of the poor in the spirit of Christ. He, they believe, was born poor to deliver the poor from tyranny and liberate them for a better earthly life in preparation for the Kingdom of Heaven. The implication here is not that the leaders or members of the communities are uninformed or naive. The point is that their first priority is raising the level of spiritual and material matters for the improvement of their religious, political, economic, social, and cultural situation.[6] Their success would represent, indeed, a direct potential threat to the domination of the ruling classes. It could also represent a threat to the official church if the methods by which results are achieved are distasteful to the conservative clergy or do not carry the hierarchy's seal of approval.

The method or effect of liberating the poor more than underlying theoretical ideologies and theologies represent the stuff of politics for the ruling oligarchies and the church, even when controversy within the church appears to be abstractly theological or about the relationship between Catholicism and Marxism.

Controversies between governments and church tend to be more openly straightforwardly political than those within the church between the traditional and the Liberation theologians. When governments complain about Marxism in the church, they refer to down-to-earth political dangers to themselves. When the official church complains about it to the Liberation theologians, the controversy assumes the form of theological discourse. It is nevertheless also political because, with Marxism being anathema, the official church is anxious about its ecclesiastic structure, internal power, and control over the Magisterium.

Unfortunately for the beneficial productivity of controversy and debate, there is much imprecision in the rhetorical postures of all concerned. A major contribution to this shortcoming is a failure to recognize or admit that Marxism and Catholicism start from two different primary concerns. For Marxism this is material liberation here and now. For the church it has traditionally been spiritual liberation until the expansion of this concept included material liberation. The church has no reason any longer to object to the principle of material liberation, nor has Marxism reason to object to spiritual liberation. Their priorities still differ. Marxism begins and ends with material liberation. The church subordinates material to spiritual liberation. There is no fundamental contradiction in this, not from the church standpoint.

Incompatibilities for both begin in the methods each proposes for reaching its goals. They differ. To make them convincing, to legitimizing them in the light of the goals, each side belittles or condemns those of the other. The church, for instance, rejects the Marxist concept of human nature, the necessity of class war, the materialist orientation, the atheism. Marxism rejects the divine origin of poverty, the surrender to a society allegedly ordained by God, the irrelevance of material existence compared to the expectation of the Kingdom of God and, resulting from all this, the passivity with which the poor are to accept their fate (the "opium of the people").

There is confusing use of concepts, of which all parties are guilty. Class is one example. It has meant sometimes workers as against owners of the means of production, sometimes rich versus poor, and sometimes oppressor versus oppressed. Revolution has been used to describe radical change, at other times violent change. Social conflict is a moral issue for the church, a matter of clashing interests for the Marxist.

For governments, Marxism signifies its historical realization in the form of totalitarian states. So, most of the time does the church consider it. The Liberation theologians distinguish between Marxism as an ideology and as a historic reality. They do not admit that the ideology must necessarily lead to a totalitarian state. Some feel justified therefore to consider it an alternative to prevailing capitalist systems. Others, including popes, see no danger in being eclectic about it. Most agree on the usefulness of Marxist methods for the analysis of societies.

All this implies that in many cases, especially in the debate within the church, conflicts may not be as substantial as they seem. Pope John Paul II appears to realize this, hence his endeavor to conciliate between the Liberation theologians and those in the Vatican opposing them.

The insistence of the Vatican upon its interpretation, especially the great reluctance to grant more importance to worldly matters, presumably follows from an attempt to keep the separation clear between

Caesar's and the church's empire. To keep out of secular politics, at least officially, seems a matter of self-preservation in a world full of totalitarian states. Paradoxically, it increases controversial internal church politics. But, as a survey of the Latin American situation will demonstrate, this may eventually simply be a detour to secular politics. Moreover, Rome's belief that internal dissenters can more easily be controlled could turn out to be an illusion, as it has been once before.

As the Latin American situation also demonstrates, Liberation Theology appears to be here to stay. Notwithstanding some dependence of its fate on bishops sympathetic or unsympathetic to the Theology in individual countries or even districts of individual countries, nowhere has it disappeared once it had followers. Pope John Paul II was seemingly ambivalent about the Theology when he was traveling through the Third World. Yet he never missed making concessions to its substance at some point. He did the same, in essence, in his encyclicals *Laborem exercens* in 1981 and *Sollicitudo rei socialis* in 1988. They may, in addition to his possible sympathy, also be indicative of a belief in the permanence of the Theology in the Third World and in the wisdom of integrating its substance into the Magisterium.

11
Latin American Churches, States, and Liberation Theology

The status of Liberation Theology varies greatly from country to country in Latin America. In Colombia, where the controlling top level of the hierarchy is unsympathetic to the Theology, it is not influential. In Brazil, where the high level hierarchy is generally sympathetic, it has a large following and by far the largest number of Ecclesiastic Base Communities. Along this spectrum, all gradations can be found. There are also some countries where Liberation Theology plays no role at all.

Quite apart from the relative novelty of the Theology, other factors could be responsible for this great diversity: the historical tradition, the nature of the political regime, the attitudes of local bishops. Pope John Paul II, as was explained earlier, during his travels through Latin America tended to support local bishops so that his position on the occasion of his visits neither added nor detracted much from whatever prevalence the theology had in the given locality.

In El Salvador, bishops, clerics, and the religious can be found in many places along the spectrum from pro- to anti-Liberation Theology. Four of six bishops have been critical of moving in the direction of Liberation Theology. One of these four is an honorary colonel in the army, another is a large landholder.[1] These bishops have criticized church support for the Christian Federation of Salvadoran Peasants, social work among the poor, and the late Archbishop Oscar Romero for supporting "marxist priests."[2] They prefer the status quo of the traditional church: separation from temporal matters and devotion to spiritual matters. They appear unwilling to combine the spiritual with the social work of the church. A minority of the clergy sides with these bishops. A similar fraction of the clergy accepts a Marxist analysis of their society but is worried about Marxist solutions of its problems, which are rejected.[3]

Under the leadership of the late Archbishop Romero and his more moderate successor Arturo Rivera y Damas, an estimated one half of the clergy were actively supporting social work among the poor and sympathetic to Liberation theology. Archbishop Romero paid for his outspoken stand with his life. He was murdered at the altar in 1980. It appears the Salvadoran government had a hand in the assassination. The more conciliatory attitude of his successor and his Auxiliary Bishop Gregorio Rosa Chavez (who is outspokenly opposed to the guerrillas and any "Marxist line" in the church) did not save them from threats to their lives.[4]

The more moderate stand of Archbishop Rivera y Damas found expression, for instance, in his reluctant approval of United States arms supplies to El Salvador to balance supplies "probably" going to the rebels. He added at once, though, that as a man of peace, he would prefer no arms supplies to any side and leaving the solution of Salvadoran problems to the Salvadorans. He was equally balanced in his even-handed distribution of relief to supporters of the government as well as the rebels. Initially, he would presumably not have justified, as did his predecessor, the violent resistance activities of the so-called rebels. Changing circumstances induced him in January 1981 to admit the moral justification under tightly prescribed conditions (following the popes) of their insurrection.[5]

This concession to the rebels allowed him to play a more effective mediating role between government and rebels, which he believed to be successful. Under his regime, some unification of church factions has taken place. His attempt to reconcile political factions has not been as successful. Altogether, he has not earned much gratitude from various quarters for his reconciliation activities.

Governmental attacks upon clergy, missionaries, and the Ecclesiastical Base Communities, or upon secular popular organizations emerging from them, have not ceased. Activities related to Liberation Theology remain risky. Some concepts of the communities, such as "reality" or "leadership," are still considered dangerous by the Salvadoran right. The Catholic Traditionalist Movement accused the archbishop of showing "class hatred" and of acting in a "diabolical communist way." It opposed peace talks as a "sterile dialogue" and a "communist farce."[6] Increasing combative activities by the rebels since 1986 have led to greater criticism of the Salvadoran church, with a corresponding decline in the archbishop's mediating function. On the other hand, the archbishop's criticism of the government in failing to take care of the poorest has not made him popular with President Duarte. When, for instance, after the 1986 earthquake, very little was done to rebuild affordable housing for the poor on the land or in the city slums, the archbishop stated, "If we want to avoid future social catastrophes, the government should concern itself primarily with the reconstruction of housing of the poorest, of the popular *barrios*, because, if not, there will not be any real reconstruction." He added "We are making a call to launch daring programs for the liberation of millions of people whose social or political repression is intolerable."[7] That call was far removed from a change in "sinful structures" or a conversion of the men in the Salvadoran government.

The U.S. government feels that under the regime of José Napoléon Duarte the country has moved toward democracy. Liberation theologian Sobrino shared this view, but qualified that the progress was toward purely "formal democracy," not the "substance of real democracy."[8] This, he felt in 1987, was partly prevented by U.S. policies which were fomenting war and aiming solely at destroying whatever was "East" in El Salvador. Later that year, Archbishop Rivero y Damas feared that the favorable development in the country had ended with the return of the death squads. His fears seemed justified when in April, 1988, the right-wing party of Robert d'Aubuisson won a stunning election victory.[9] The optimism of the U.S. State Department was hardly justified that the United States "had consistently supported democratization to successful outcomes."[10]

In Nicaragua, the situation is more opaque. It is clear only that the pace of progress of the poor is slowing down. In the civil war, the factionalism within the church, the state-church disputes, the international interventions, few people can be objective in evaluating the situation. The government is in conflict with the institutionalized church and favors a People's church, whose very existence some members of the clergy deny. Other clergy, identifying themselves with a People's church are not sympathetic to the Sandinista regime. The contras considered the Ecclesiastic Base Communities favorite targets for attack.[11] Growing numbers of Protestant and fundamentalist groups, originating mostly in the United States, are hostile to the Sandinistas and all Catholics alike. The Liberation theologians have the sympathy of the Soviet Union,[12] but deny any communist influence or subversion of the Base Communities. In fact, the argument has been made by clergy and laypersons alike, that the presence of priests in the government prevents subversion by communism.

The public is described as confused and neighborhoods as split. The believers, more interested in praying than politicking, often go to the church or priest of their choice, where the factionalism plays a more subordinate role, or they abandon religion altogether.

When the Somoza regime was ousted in July 1979, the church welcomed the revolution at the last moment, then changed to coolness and finally to outright opposition. In a pastoral letter of the Nicaraguan bishops November 17, 1979, their fundamental view of the relations between the official church and the Sandinista government was outlined.[13] It was a balanced statement welcoming the revolution and the opportunities it could bring to eliminate oppression and create a "new man." It also warned of potential risks and dangers of the revolutionary process unless the revolutionaries would keep their promise to choose the legal route. "We believe that the present revolutionary moment is a favorable opportunity to realize the ecclesiastical option for the poor." It even welcomed socialism if that meant primacy of the interests of the majority of the people and a solidaristic, increasingly participatory and nationwide economic model, compatible with religious faith. The "liberation in Jesus Christ" included, according to the letter, the satisfaction of the most elementary human needs and an economic structure in the service of man, leading to a just society. The first contribution of the church would be its partisanship in favor of the poor. All the church demanded was freedom to complete its apostolic work. The people must revive its vital force in an increasingly more brotherly fashion, "above all in the Ecclesiastic Base Communities."

On October 7, 1980, the National Directorate of the Sandinista Liberation Front published a document in which the positive influence of Christians in the revolutionary struggle and process was acknowledged and religious freedom was guaranteed. It did not fail to mention opposition by some Christians to the revolution and warned that if ever religious ceremonies or festivals were to be used as a cover for counterrevolutionary activity, the revolutionaries would defend themselves. The document also praised the cooperation of priests and religious in the government, declaring at the same time they would be free to withdraw whenever their conscience told them to do so.

The forecast of possible friction soon came true. In August 1983, a commission from CIDSE, an international working group of 13 Catholic organizations engaged in development work, found it appropriate to make a comprehensive survey of the situation. It concluded,[14] among other things, that the church was split in regard to support of or opposition to the "revolutionary process." Among the supporters could be found the "majority" of eight hundred members of religious orders working in Nicaragua in some research and educational institutes, in the government, and in the few Ecclesiastical Base Communities. Some church groups were found to fear the turning of the revolution toward totalitarianism, although the surveying group found no restriction upon religious freedom. Among the outright opposition were found to be three of eight bishops, the archbishop of Managua being among the three; some priests and members of religious orders; some Christian organizations; and individual Christians.

The "overwhelming majority" of Catholics, the survey found, did not participate in these "diverging options" and took no sides. In the eyes of this majority of "traditional Latin American Catholics" bishops and priests were sacred and attacks upon them were condemned. But this same majority "recognizes the actual value" of the revolutionary process and participated in it. Unfortunately, the survey ended, there was no dialogue among all these contending factions, and no institution to initiate it. Tensions and splits were found to be greater than at the beginning of the revolution. They showed no abating as time went on. The parties were confronting each other with increasing hostility.

The findings of the commission were confirmed openly very soon. In 1983, Bishop Antonio Vega, president of the Nicaraguan Bishops Conference, branded the government "Marxist-Leninist" because of its "ideology and method," but he nevertheless called for conciliation during his invocation at the inauguration of President Ortega in 1985. Cardinal Obando y Bravo described the Sandinistas as totalitarian Marxists and enemies of the church. He is considered the rallying point of opposition to the Sandinistas although he is also reputed to be opposed more to revolution than some form of liberalism.

In the summer of 1984 he addressed businessmen in New York, claiming to have the best organized campaign against the intrusion of communists into the church. His activities, he stressed, were not political. He was training "pastoral cadres," not military cadres. In the past, he said, he had received help from the U.S. Agency for International Development, but not in recent years. He expressed the hope of receiving financial help from those he addressed and he assured them that he had distanced himself from the Sandinistas in 1979 and was eager to see their government removed. Again in 1985 Cardinal Obando, and in the first half of 1986 Bishop Vega, traveled to the United States. The cardinal addressed a number of right-wing groups and during a mass in Miami blessed the contras and their supporters.[15]

Bishop Vega twice lobbied in Washington for support to the contras during the House voting on that question. He also accused the Sandinista government of trying to split the Catholic church and paying—directly or indirectly—clergymen for developing a parallel church. He supplied President Reagan with arguments in favor of contra help. During meetings in Washington and elsewhere he called for "armed struggle" to overthrow the Sandinista government.[16] On July 4, 1986, he was not allowed to return to Nicaragua, the government arguing that deportation was more humane than trying him for treason. Thereafter, he spent much time traveling across the United States and other nations to argue for contra help because he felt that "military activity should continue." Eventually, he was called to Rome and effectively silenced. While the bishop was abroad, his colleague in Managua, Monsignor Bismarck Carballo, continued his attacks on the Sandinista government until he, too, was banned in 1986 from the country and continued his activities from the United States.

The agency of the cardinal receiving and disbursing funds in support of activities by the "traditional" church is the Commission for Social Promotion (COPROS), founded in 1980. Spokesmen for the organization asserted that it was concerned only with "humanitarian services and spiritual formation," not with politics. They admitted that in obedience to the church hierarchy and devotion to family and spiritual matters, COPROS countered the political and pro-Sandinista activities of the People's church. Government sources claimed COPROS was one of the CIA instruments in its Nicaraguan counterrevolutionary work.

Obando's position as cardinal provides him with considerable influence on his country's clergy as well as that of Central America in general. Nevertheless, his attempts to make the clergy declare itself for or against the Sandinista government and then to isolate those opting for the government has not been entirely successful.[17] Gary MacEoin reported in 1984 that a survey of 220 priests in 1983 showed 54 percent opposed to the Sandinistas. Religious and foreign missionaries tended to share this opposition. Diocesan and native-born priests tended to be more sympathetic to the government. Many members of the clergy argued that the government was there to stay. The church should find a way to coexist. In later years, this proportion of pro versus con did not appear to have undergone much change. Some missionaries described the poor as confused, unable to understand why the church was opposing the Sandinista government from which they felt they had benefited so much.

By 1984, the relationships between the official church, Liberation theologians, and the Sandinista government had further deteriorated. Within the official Nicaraguan church, some sections of the clergy considered themselves a political opposition to the government,[18] while another cooperated with the revolutionaries. This division then was reflected in the attitude of bishops toward the Ecclesiastical Base Communities.

After the revolution, some bishops were concerned about how the communities would affect the unity of the church. They harbored doubts concerning where the loyalties of the communities really lay—whether with the revolution or the church. Close relations of some communities with secular pro-Sandinista popular organizations, whose leaders sometimes originated in the communities, reinforced these doubts. Attempts by some bishops to gain control over the communities and dam their politicization caused resentment over "interference." Other bishops helped and protected them. The cardinal in Managua criticized what he felt was the attempt of the local communities to renew the society rather than the church.[19]

At the same time, the conflict between the official Nicaraguan church and the government sharpened.[20] On April 22, 1984, the Nicaraguan bishops published a pastoral letter "On Reconciliation." They reconfirmed it in March 1985. The letter described the unhappy situation in the country. It complained about a "small sector of the church which has abandoned ecclesiastical unity" and "surrendered to the tenets of materialistic ideology. This sector throws confusion inside and outside Nicaragua through a campaign extolling its own ideas and defaming the legitimate pastors and the faithful who follow them. Censorship of the media makes it impossible to clarify the positions and offer other points of view." The letter then suggested reconciliation and a dialogue in which all Nicaraguans, those within and without the country, must participate.

This suggestion was rejected by the government and several church groups. Among these were Jesuits trying to demonstrate that neither on historical nor religious grounds was the suggestion for unconditional forgiveness and reconciliation reasonable or justifiable.

This pastoral letter was followed by polemical statements from both sides. Tomas Borge, a Cabinet member, called these bishops "a race of traitors" belonging to the sector of the church that had turned itself over to imperialism. A few months later he added "all we ask from them is that they teach the Gospel and spread God's word, and that they not plot against the revolution or accept the CIA's money." Archbishop (later cardinal) Obando in June 1984 accused the government of using Marxism to eliminate the church "in order to implant the so-called Popular Church" and continued in his anti-Sandinista campaign.

The presence of ten clergy and religious in the Sandinista government, of whom three are ministers, has become a focus of the religious and political controversy, involving to some extent Liberation Theology also. Great pressure has been exerted upon them by Nicaraguan clerics to resign, by the Vatican and, through the Vatican, by Washington. They have refused to do so, because they considered such a step a betrayal of the people's trust.[21]

Father Fernando Cardenal, minister for education, was expelled from the Jesuit Order on December 10, 1984, and suspended from priestly duties by express order of the pope, allegedly because the order itself refused to do so.[22] Technically, he was in violation of canon law, forbidding priests to perform official political functions. The Nicaraguan bishops had granted him exemption from this rule, but had refused to renew it. In a deeply religious statement, Father Cardenal justified his refusal to abandon his government position. He left no doubt that in his opinion his suspension was not due to canon law but to politics and opposition to Liberation Theology. "I believe the Vatican has been influenced too much by its experience. We are not Poles. The Vatican is incapable of recognizing anything new unless it comes from Europe." He declared that he was at peace because he felt he was doing God's will and because the Society of Jesus had understood "that I am acting out of conscience."[23] He added, in 1985, that he did not think there was incompatibility between Christianity and Marxism. "One can be a Marxist without being an atheist." Christianity and Marxism both preach mutual love among men, justice, fraternity, and equality, he added.

Father Miguel d'Escoto, foreign minister, had already been suspended from his priestly duties in 1981. Early in 1985 the Vatican asked him once again to resign as minister. The pope also asked Maryknoll General J. P. Noonan to dismiss d'Escoto from the Order. But the general refused to do so, explaining, "I am a North American. The North Americans attack unjustly Nicaragua. In this situation, I cannot expel Escoto."[24] In July and August 1985, d'Escoto engaged in an *insurreccion evangélica* by means of a hunger strike and a 400-kilometer Way of the Cross to protest American "terrorism" and Archbishop Obando's political posture.[25] His insurrection elicited sympathetic support from various quarters of the world. The Brazilian socialist Bishop Pedro Casaldágila flew to Managua to go on a sympathy hunger strike with d'Escoto. The Nicaraguan Bishops Conference protested his "unwarranted interference" in Nicaraguan church affairs and Brazil's bishops were divided along several lines in their reaction to Casaldágila's action.[26]

In September 1984, a delegation of the Nicaraguan government held several conferences in the Vatican in an attempt to solve some of the problems between the government and the official church. The only public result was a nondescript communiqué. The delegation repeated the government's willingness to let the three ministers decide for themselves what they wanted to do, but complained about the politicization of the official Nicaraguan church. They pointed out that the church had sent home 52 foreign priests who supported the Sandinistas, while the church had never criticized the Somoza regime. In 1985, President Ortega was trying to enlist Cardinal Obando's help in mediating the many conflicts producing Nicaragua's difficult position. But all attempts at reconciliation seemed condemned to failure. A wide gap continued to separate the government from the Vatican and differences within the Nicaraguan clergy sharpened.

Beginning in the fall of 1985—and allegedly as a countermeasure to U.S. support of the contras—the Sandinista government became increasingly restrictive in general and regarding the official Catholic church in particular. The church complained about threats, intimidation, censorship, harassment, persecution, and interference with its followers. In January 1985, Cardinal Obando asked the Secretary General of the United Nations for intervention on behalf of the church. The *Osservatore Romano* in January 1986 accused the government of wanting to suffocate the liberty of the church in order to suffocate the liberty of an entire population.[27] Three months later, a letter from the bishops accused the People's church of seeking "to manipulate the basic truth of the faith."

Monsignor Carballo added that "The prophetic church is built for and with the poor, but the popular church is being built from the desks in air-conditioned offices."[28] Father Miguel d'Escoto was accused of trying to provoke an insurrection of Catholics against the pope and the Nicaraguan hierarchy.[29] (He supported Argentina during the Falkland war, though contras had trained some of Argentina's forces. This, he said, was "a matter of the heart.")[30]

The government replied that its suppressive actions were caused by and targeted at purely political antigovernment activities of the church; freedom of religion was not affected by any official measures.[31] These actions eventually included the closing down of the Catholic radio station and of the independent newspaper *La Prensa*. When Bishop Vega was prevented from returning to Nicaragua from the United States, the Nicaraguan bishops wrote to several Bishops Conferences in several parts of the world, asking them to protest. A number of Third World bishops decided to investigate the situation on the spot. Each of them wrote a report and all came to about the same conclusions: They praised the freedom allowed them to move around the country and make contacts with any individuals they wished to interview; there was no religious persecution or curtailment of church freedom; there was no evidence of communist subversion; on the contrary, opposition parties were permitted, Protestant sects proliferated, and private organizations were active without any restrictions. At about the same time, Juan Manuel Pérez, Secretary General of the Dominican Order, also denied the existence of religious persecution "in the most absolute manner." Cardinal Danneels of Belgium stated that he saw no socialism during his travels through Central America.[32]

There was hope that the tense relationships between state and church would come to an end when, in August 1987, five Central American states signed the "peace treaty" proposed by the Contadora group. The U.S. government called it a good beginning, but leaving much to be done yet. The Soviet Union welcomed it as providing an opportunity to solve the conflicts in Latin America and give each of the signatories a chance for social and economic improvements.

In an attempt to improve the atmosphere before the signing of the treaty, and thereafter to show goodwill toward fulfillment of it, President Ortega permitted the return of Bishop Vega and Monsignor Caballo. In the fall of 1987, the Catholic radio station was permitted to broadcast again and *La Prensa* reappeared, the radio station only to be silenced, again in July, 1988, and *La Prensa*'s publication to be suspended for two weeks. But the 18 priests expelled by the government were not yet allowed to return. A conciliation committee was appointed by President Ortega, in fulfillment of the treaty terms, with the task of arranging for a cease-fire between Sandinistas and contras. An amnesty in Managua was declared, and an agreement on democratic reforms was proposed. Ortega appointed Cardinal Obando as head of the committee and later agreed to having the cardinal serve as an intermediary between the Sandinistas and the contras. In early March 1988, Ortega proposed direct talks with the contras. Their initial result was agreement on a truce, to begin April 1, 1988, and to last for two months. The hope was that peace would result from these negotiations. President Reagan ordered the CIA to end its role as guide and chief supplier to the contras and placed the Agency for International Development in charge of the "humanitarian" aid to the contras.

The meetings between President Ortega and Cardinal Obando made fairly clear that the government's aim was depoliticization of the church, while the church was aiming at greater autonomy, symbolized, for instance, by its insistence upon the return of the 18 expelled priests, none of whom was reported as sympathetic to Liberation Theology.

This expulsion of priests by one or the other side in the conflict played an important concrete and symbolic role. The church claimed at one time that the government had expelled 30 priests and religious from the country because of their anti-Sandinista sympathies, while the Sandinistas claimed that the church had sent some 200 priests and religious out of the country because they were suspected of Sandinista and Liberation Theology sympathies. In April 1986, the Vatican, upon Cardinal Obando's request, recalled its nuncio from Managua, allegedly for being too close to the Sandinistas. He was replaced later by a nuncio who was said to be more neutral and better qualified as a mediator between government and church.[33] The issue of expelling priests from the country had reached a high point in April 1986 when the Franciscan Father Uriel Molina was asked by his religious superiors to leave Nicaragua. He was suspected of sympathy for the Sandinistas, and he asked "is this persecution of the church or by the church?" Eventually, he was allowed to stay.[34]

From the beginning of the revolution, multifaceted conflicts within Nicaragua have escalated. The confrontation between the government and the Catholic hierarchy involved ideologies and politics of such opposite character that a compromise was difficult to envisage. The Vatican's cautious intervention aggravated the confrontation and the splits within the clergy. The siding of the United States with the contras, and thereby with the official church, further complicated the issues. All of these are immixed with the passions of the civil war at the expense of rational settlements. The leadership of all the factions is so preoccupied by the conflicts that religion and the poor are neglected. Followers of the official church fail to attend services. Protestantism and fundamentalism are making significant inroads with the help of U.S. money. Opponents of Liberation Theology are gaining with the help also of German money. The Ecclesiastic Base Communities are stagnating.[35] The government's ability to assist the poor is severely curtailed. It cannot be made up by the Witnesses for Peace and other private organizations working in the countryside.

Ironically, in the country whose government has generated changes bringing the society closer to the elimination of "sinful structures," the official church is highly critical of the government. Obviously, the changes the government introduced did not appeal to the church. But possibly also, the rejection of the government by the church resulted from the failure of the church to outline what structures might achieve the desired result. Its frequent criticism of capitalism as being too materialistic, as overemphasizing the profit motive, as being callous to human aspects of employer-worker relations are integral elements of the system. If conversion of individuals or governments were to be successful in eliminating these features, the system would no longer be capitalist. But since the church also rejects socialist systems, the question remains unanswered, that is, just what alternative the church envisages?

In Guatemala,[36] the Catholic church is confronted by the unusual situation in Latin America that only about 60 percent of the population are Catholic. In 1982 General Efrain Rios Montt came to power, a reborn Protestant Christian who preached his evangelical faith and persecuted members of the Catholic clergy and followers. He kept them under the strictest supervision and many were being killed on the merest suspicion or denunciation. Social work by Catholics was attacked as communist and subversive. Some of these workers were accused, and correctly so, of fighting with the "rebels" against the government in an endeavor to relieve the unbearable conditions of the poor. Many Catholic programs had to be halted because poor people were afraid of leaving their houses in the evening—the only time they had to attend meetings. It was "not healthy" to be a missionary, wrote one of them.[37] The government was suspected of trying to split the Catholic church by dividing it into "good" and "bad" wings, reminiscent of the "Banzer" plan of 1957 (a CIA-inspired and sponsored program, beginning in Bolivia but designed for all Latin America, to sow discord in the Catholic church and discredit individual, especially progressive, clerics.)[38]

The effort was not unsuccessful until the pope visited Guatemala in 1983. His presence strengthened a trend that had resulted from the church's persecution by the government. A new sense of certainty and confidence as well as hope seemed to have awakened in Guatemala's Catholics. In 1983, military leaders decided to rescue Guatemala from internal turmoil and international isolation by transferring the government to civilians. In January 1986, the Christian Democrat (left of center) Vinicio Cerezo was inaugurated as president. He was reputed to be a moderate, fair-minded person, but has, so far, not been able to assume full control of the country which remained largely in the hands of the military. While murders, kidnapping and disappearances of persons have greatly diminished, they have not ceased. In 1986 four Catholic catechists and activists were kidnapped by the Army. At least two have been found dead; the fate of the others was unknown. Among the four were members of Base Communities and the Indian community.[39]

The Indians, in particular, suffered and still suffer from persecution. At the same time the work of the Base Communities was most successful among them. It is the only institution helping them to survive. It has changed their way of life in the distant parts of Guatemala to where they have fled. They have created communities coming close to primitive communism, or better communalism, and they have developed a new sense of being Christians. President Cerezo is not encouraging them, but at the same time, he is not fighting them. There can be little doubt that these Indian communities are coming closest to what the official church, rhetorically, and the Liberation theologians, actively, are trying to achieve for the poor masses. However, the insecure conditions under which the Catholic church exists in Guatemala absorbs its attention and politics. There is little time left to deal extensively with the problems of the poor, or especially the bitter fate of the Indians. Liberation Theology does not have a high priority in Guatemala.

Colombia is the country in which Liberation Theology got its first foothold. But that was in the 1960s. Since then, the country has become the battleground for innumerable groups, ranging from the army to roving bands of killers, turning it to virtual anarchy. In 1986 alone, for different reasons, some 11,000 citizens were killed. Among them were priests, human rights activists, labor union leaders and professors, as well as drug traffickers, prostitutes, peasants, and their leaders. There was no pattern in these killings. Each group killed its own enemies. But generally speaking, individuals of the political left (of center) represented the most victims and much of the money for the killers came from large landowners and major drug smugglers.

Liberation Theology began, though not under that name, with Camilo Torres. After sociology studies at Louvain, he worked with the poor in Colombia, gave up his priestly function, and became a revolutionary on the ground of practicing "love for people in temporal, economic and social spheres." He fell in combat on the guerrilla side in 1966. Following the Medellín and Puebla conferences, Ecclesiastic Base Communities also developed in Colombia. But the murder of numerous priests, nuns, and religious between 1980 and 1987 was not restricted to Liberation theologians, their followers, or the communities.[40] All those who subscribed to the conclusions of the conferences became targets of military or paramilitary forces as being too progressive.

Following the publication of Pope Pius VI's encyclical *Populorum progressio,* 1967, Third World bishops had drawn up a statement more radical than the pope's encyclical. Groups of priests in various Latin American countries, including Colombia, took this statement as the basis for creating a Movement of Priests for the Third World, whose members were mostly those working closest to the poor people and advocating a more frugal existence for church and clergy. From these groups came a considerable percentage of followers of Liberation Theology and Base Community workers. But under the conditions as they developed in Colombia, Liberation Theology, the Base Communities, and land reforms had little chance to develop. In early 1988, reports from Colombia still talked of "close ties" between the ruling class (or one might better say *classes*) and the official church. With Cardinal Trujillo in control of the Colombian official church, it was predictable that the popular church and the Base Communities would lose all independence. The cardinal saw to it that unity in the church would be interpreted in the most traditional fashion. For the communities this meant their subjection to clerical control and, at least overtly, adherence to orthodox ideology. The authoritarian government combined with the authoritarian nature of the Colombia hierarchy make the country most inhospitable to Liberation Theology and Base Communities. Insistence of the hierarchy, headed by Cardinal Trujillo, upon orthodox adherence to the tightest vertical organization of the church robs progressive Catholics of all freedom of open action.[41]

In Peru,[42] the homeland of Gutiérrez, the fate of Liberation Theology had been greatly affected by the ups and downs of various factions in the Peruvian official church. But it started with the distinct advantage that Ecclesiastical Base Communities were already in existence when the Theology became a subject of discussion in Peru.

In the past, the Peruvian hierarchy had the reputation of being quite unsophisticated and subservient to the Vatican.[43] In 1968 the civilian government was overthrown by General Juan Velasco Alvarado. His government introduced a number of liberal social reforms and the Medellín Conference took place. Whether or not as a result, the Peruvian bishops changed their position and issued a pastoral letter supportive of socialism. The overthrow of General Velasco in 1975 by a more conservative general did not affect the Peruvian bishops' commitment to the poor or their work in the slums and with peasant organizations. Liberation Theology supplied the ecclesiastical foundation for these activities—although a priest working in the slums of Lima stated in 1985 that the issue for him and the poor was daily survival, not theology—was, in other words, not the pursuit of the higher goals of Liberation Theology, especially not conscientization.

The pastoral letter on socialism initiated a conservative reaction in the early 1970s, aiming at weakening the influence of the more progressive bishops, especially Archbishop Juan, Cardinal Ricketts Landázuri, and a few others. The cardinal was publicly attacked as a sympathizer with, if not an adherent of Marxism. He was, however, generally credited with considerable influence upon Pope John Paul II and of having saved Gutiérrez from being silenced by the Vatican. He also appeared to have been instrumental having the pope suggesting the softening of a document the Peruvian bishops were asked to produce on Liberation Theology. The story of this document is important for understanding Peru's location in the Liberation Theology controversy; also as providing a glimpse into the inner workings of the church.

In March 1983, Cardinal Ratzinger, as Prefect of the Sacred Congregation for the Doctrine of the Faith, sent the Peruvian bishops a statement containing ten charges against Gutiérrez's theology. Most of them dealt with the "Marxist" reinterpretation and "perversion" of the Bible, the Christian message, and the hierarchical organization of the Catholic church.[44] Gutiérrez submitted a reply, 60 pages long, in June. In plenary session, the Bishops' Council in August 1983 and January 1984 condemned the theologian's writings, but failed to agree on the statement Cardinal Ratzinger requested. A commission of six was chosen. Five of them turned out to be sympathetic to Liberation Theology, so two more were added for the sake of "balance." They travelled to Rome and in cooperation with the Congregation for the Doctrine of the Faith drew up a document to be used for the required statement. Shortly thereafter, in September 1984, all Peruvian bishops traveled to Rome. They found the document unacceptable. Eighteen bishops wanted to condemn Gutiérrez, 18 did not, and 17 abstained.[45] Cardinal Landázuri, it was reported, persuaded the pope to address the assembled bishops on social justice. The unacceptable document was then replaced by another, more general in tone and not specifically directed at Peru. The bishops agreed that they could "live with it." This second document omitted a section headed "erroneous Opinions," referring to passages from the theologian's writings, and much less harsh in tone than the first document. It was published in Peru on November 24, 1984.

Deep concern for the poor was expressed in a rather tortuous fashion in the document. Some forms of Liberation Theology were approved. Marxism and class war were severely condemned. Although the document called itself *Documento de la conferencia Episcopal Peruana sobre la teología de la liberación*[46] it failed to deal with it squarely and was open to a variety of interpretations.

Under the leadership of the conservative Archbishop Fernando Vargas Ruiz, a competing and opposing "theology of reconciliation and dialogue" was being promoted in Peru (and elsewhere), or at least was intended to compete with Liberation Theology. Gutiérrez called it a "joke" because he saw no contrast between Liberation Theology and a reconciliation in the Christian sense—which is different from a social reconciliation that was not the issue.[47]

As the number of conservative bishops had increased, the long-run trend in the Peruvian church was likely to be against Liberation Theology. It also seemed to be true, as Penny Lernoux reported, that even for the leftist intellectuals, social change is a trickle-down process from the top to the bottom in Peru.[48] The Base Communities are therefore of interest to them mainly as supplying votes, not as participants in the political process shaping the history of their own members. For any change in the social "sinful structure" the situation does not look promising.

Brazil is the homeland of Leonardo Boff. It is also the country in which Liberation Theology, the Ecclesiastic Base Communities, and the People's church are most firmly rooted. The majority of the hierarchy, among them Aloisio Cardinal Lorscheider, Paulo Cardinal Evaristo Arns, and Archbishop Ivo Lorscheiter actively support Liberation Theology. The elections of the National Conference of Brazilian Bishops in the spring of 1987 confirmed the liberal trend within the hierarchy. The three highest officers were progressives or moderate progressives. Similarly, members representing progressives or moderate progressives formed the majority in the Episcopal Pastoral Council. The Brazilian delegates to CELAM, the Latin American episcopal conference, also were progressives who could look forward to some disputes within CELAM, since Cardinal Alfonso Lopez Trujillo of Colombia has a major conservative influence.

During the years of rule by a military dictatorship (1964-1985) the progressive elements in the church, especially those subscribing to Liberation Theology, were in trouble with the dictatorship as well as the Vatican. The military dictatorship ended in 1986, but conflict with the Vatican did not. The progressives in the Brazilian church and their Liberation Theology became the favorite target of the Vatican. It had the cooperation of Cardinal Trujillo—who once vowed to "smash" the Brazilian bishops—and of the conservative Brazilian bishops who admitted being in a "shrinking" minority but promised the world they would do all they could. They did not succeed in preventing the election of progressives to almost all the offices of the National Conference of Brazilian Bishops in 1987.[49]

In early 1984, the conservative Cardinal Eugenio Sales dismissed

Clodovis Boff (Leonardo's brother) and the theologian Antonio Moser from the papal University of Rio de Janeiro for using "marxist thought categories." At the same time, five faculty members of the Department of Theology at the University of the Ursulines in Rio were also dismissed.

Early in 1984, the Vatican sent the late archbishop of Cologne, Joseph Cardinal Höffner to São Paulo, Brazil's most important diocese, to "inspect" Cardinal Arns' work. He performed his task in such an unpleasant manner that the ten auxiliary bishops of the diocese carried a strong letter of protest to Rome, with other clergy joining their protest.[50]

The "Boff case" (to be discussed later) proved very upsetting to the Brazilian clergy. When Boff was silenced by the Vatican from April 1985 to March 1986 for criticizing the organization of the official church, its monopoly and misuse of power, the Commission on the Faith of the Brazilian Bishops Conference met (boycotted by Cardinal Sales and Bishop Romer). The conference expressly supported Boff and insisted—without success—that Boff's conversations with Cardinal Ratzinger should take place in Brazil. They feared the case as symbolic for an attack upon Liberation Theology and designed to increase tensions in the Brazilian clergy. However, on the second point, the Brazilian Bishop Erwin Krautler affirmed that the bishops always agreed on important questions by an "overwhelming majority." Moreover, as Cardinal Arns' advisor, Pater Gilberto Gorgulho, stated confidently that Liberation Theology was so firmly embedded in Brazil that criticism from the outside "carried little weight."[51] Nevertheless, the fears were not entirely unfounded.

In 1980, Pope John Paul II had told the Brazilian bishops not to substitute the Base Communities for the parishes and to consider the Vatican's Congregation for the Doctrine of the Faith (i.e. Cardinal Ratzinger) as if it were the pope. Since then, an element of uneasiness beclouded Vatican–Brazilian church relations. However, a number of events in quick succession indicated a readiness of Pope John Paul II to give the Liberation theologians in Brazil a freer hand than Cardinal Ratzinger was willing to do.

One of these events was the planned publication of 54 volumes under the general title "Theology and Liberation" in Latin America. The 115 authors were to be representative of Liberation Theology and comprise the most important Latin American authors, including some Protestants. The intellectual leaders of the enterprise are Leonardo Boff and Jon Sobrino. The project worried the Vatican because Liberation Theology would be propagated and the Western world had nothing comparable to offer since Thomas Aquinas. Cardinal Ratzinger was reported to have forbidden the publishing houses Voces in Petrópolis and Ediciones Paulinas in Buenos Aires to proceed with the publication of the available manuscripts. Thereupon, in Rome in 1986, prominent Brazilian clergy confronted Cardinal Ratzinger, in the presence of the pope, accusing him of stonewalling. Ratzinger's conditions for publication proved unacceptable to the Brazilians and the pope sided with them. The compromise result was that a commission of three Brazilian bishops would vouch for the compatibility of the books with Catholic doctrine and no Protestants would participate. But when the first two volumes were to be presented to the Bishop of Assisi, he refused to accept them.[52]

Another event was the visit of 21 Brazilian bishops to Rome for a meeting with the pope to "clear the air" over a number of "misunderstandings." Among the agenda items for the three-day meeting was the proportion of religious to mundane activities in the Brazilian church; the nature of Liberation Theology; and the activities of individual clergymen (e.g. Dom Pedro Casaldágila joining d'Escoto in his hunger strike). The meetings took place in the presence of Cardinal Ratzinger and other heads of Congregations. They ended by the pope telling the bishops that they should proceed with their programs to solve social problems but "without ambiguities and deformations" regarding Catholic doctrine. "Purified of elements which can water it down, with grave consequences for the faith, liberation theology is not only orthodox but necessary."[53] The pope added that a theological reflection on Liberation Theology should include questions of local, national, and international concern, such as justice, peace and disarmament, and human rights.

These encouraging remarks seemed contradicted by the pope's warning about Liberation Theology at about the same time, July 1986, in Bogotá, Colombia. The explanation might be, as usual, the Pope's conciliatory concern for local differences. Colombia is the home of Cardinal Trujillo where considerable restraints are placed upon Ecclesiastic Base Communities and Catholic progressivism in general.

A third great event was the publication of the *Instruction on Christian Freedom and Liberation* (March 22, 1986)—previously submitted to Brazilian and other bishops for their comments—in which Liberation Theology fared considerably better than in the 1984 *Instruction on Certain Aspects of the "Theology of Liberation"*.

The next event, a week later, was the lifting of the ban silencing Leonardo Boff. And on April 9, 1986, finally, the pope wrote a letter to the Brazilian bishops calling them "examples for all the other bishops in the world," and expressed his wish "to share with you our desire to support you and your dear basic Christian Communities. . . . You have performed an inestimable service for the church of Brazil and, beyond that, for other churches and the universal church; a service which helps indirectly Brazilian society and, beyond that, the entire human family."[54]

The encouragement was pronounced and unequivocal. The Brazilian bishops interpreted it as a shift in the pope's attitude. He ignored Cardinal

Trujillo's advice against Liberation Theology; disregarded conservative Bishop Sales' counsel; and rejected Cardinal Ratzinger's contention that episcopal conferences have no theological status or mandate to teach.

The progressive Brazilian bishops felt elated. The clergy expressed openly increasing impatience with the very slow and narrow progress of promised reforms.[55] Cardinal Lorscheider called the government, though it is in principle sympathetic to the liberalism of the church, totalitarian and fascist. Clergymen began to support or even initiate the occupation of land by peasants, provoking the organization of land-owners to resume the old custom of using violent methods against the peasants.[56] At the end of 1987, the point was reached where the National Security Council accused the bishops of interfering in state affairs by exploiting social inequalities and the difficulties of the people, of "incitement of the rural workers to land invasions and encouragement of workers to passive resistance and open rebellion." The bishops, in turn, defended their Catholic social action program, claiming that the social change they favored was based "on great moral and religious values."[57]

Antagonism was growing between the Brazilian church and the government of President Sarney and the parliament, much to the chagrin of Cardinal Sales, who felt more comfortable on the government's than the progressive bishops' side.[58] Cardinal Arns blamed the merger of voting for the constituent and the parliamentary assembly into one election for the delay in doing something for the poor. In its present form, he declared, the assembly could devote itself fully to neither assuming the people's rights in a new Constitution, nor, therefore, to implementing these rights. In the meantime, it appeared that the sharp criticism by the progressive section of the church had begun even to trouble some liberal forces in Brazil who were accusing it of wanting to take over the government of the country.

As usual in such situations, the real sufferers were the poor who have to be satisfied largely with the help coming from the Base Communities which, while numerous and widely supported in Brazil, have nevertheless only limited capabilities. Yet, as in so many other countries of Latin America, the tensions between the progressive church leaders and governments are really caused mostly by the unfulfilled promises of even fairly liberal governments to bring about substantial changes in the social system for the benefit of the poor.

Chile[59] has been among the countries in Latin America pioneering greater equality of income and opportunity for the people.[60] The public became accustomed to making government and political parties responsible for social welfare. This tradition lightened the burden of the church and other agencies in their devotion to social improvements, but did not eliminate it. Different governments took different approaches to the social problems, some much more favorable than others. The church was obliged to adjust its social work accordingly.

The church and the Liberation theologians had to live through three different regimes since Vatican II. Under President Eduardo Frei's (1964-1970) "middle of the road" policies great hopes were raised for substantial reforms. Many were realized, but not all, especially not those for a redistribution of land. Yet, the prospect of success of Frei and his Christian Democratic government attracted a great number of individuals who had previously been active in Catholic Action or would otherwise have worked in religious social agencies. The result was a public focus much more on the activities of political institutions than the church.[61]

As 1970 approached, the political left agitated for more fundamental reforms in favor of the poorest. In a parallel move, the clergy sponsored the creation of Ecclesiastic Base Communities. Their main mission was to be evangelical, but they were also to devote themselves to social and economic improvements among the poor.

When socialist Salvador Allende and his Popular Unity coalition were elected to office in 1970, two developments took place weakening the bishops' efforts further. One was the absorption of the Chilean people's interest by politics. The other was the preemption of the church's social program by the government. There also were the "Christians for Socialism," going into the communities, urging them to participate in Chile's transition toward socialism, calling for a new, less centralized church and criticizing the church for not supporting the Allende government more forcefully. The church, in turn, criticized those Catholics calling for stronger church support of the Popular Unity coalition. Such activity, the bishops argued, would identify the church with one partisan movement and destroy its universal mission with its transcendent spiritual message.

Here again, the question arose, however, of how the church proposed to introduce structural changes when it distanced itself—to avoid partisanship—from those governments most likely to produce them? The Peruvian bishops had an answer, which they forwarded to the bishops' synod in Rome in 1971. "When governments arise which are trying to implant more just and human societies in their countries, we propose that the Church commit itself to giving them its backing; contributing to the elimination of prejudice; recognizing the aspirations they hold; and encouraging the search for their own road toward a socialist society."[62]

A military coup brought General Augusto Pinochet into power in September, 1973. A majority of bishops considered the coup necessary.[63] A bloody regime of suppression was inaugurated. As was to be expected, extremely conservative policies were initiated. A precipitous decline in social expenditures took place. Land, taken from large landowners under Allende's reform program, was returned to the former owners. The government subscribed to the trickle-down theory: support industry, commerce, big agricultural enterprises. Eventually a share of their gains will trickle down to the masses. Contrary to the theory, however, taking care of the rich did not help the poor. They increased in numbers and became poorer. As most private organizations were either closed or brought under strict government control, the task of saving the lives of political opponents and taking care of the poor fell upon the only private institutions remaining formally free of government control: the religious organizations.

In October 1973, an ecumenical organization was established to coordinate relief for the needy and a refuge for the persecuted. A month later, another organization was created, with the main task of legal help to the victims of the regime and material support for their families. Base Communities sprung up in many places and suddenly assumed a new popularity. Naturally, as the clientele of the new organization was mostly opponents of the regime, it was finally closed by the government at the end of 1975. Almost immediately, the Catholic church set up a new, Catholic organization, the Vicariate of Solidarity.

The Vicariate over the years has helped hundreds of thousands of Chileans in almost every conceivable sphere: law, nutrition, health, housing, education, training, and employment. Since it used Base Communities as the fundamental units to dispense its help, they increased greatly in numbers and in importance to the people, mostly of the poorer population, but also many of the middle class. Nevertheless, the Ecclesiastical Base Communities were still in an "underdeveloped" stage. They catered to a relatively small percentage of the population. And their social activities were considerably more popular than their religious activities. This situation led to differences within the clergy on two points: first the usual one of spiritual versus mundane activity in the communities and, second, the nature of the religion that the communities should adopt: popular religion or more orthodox Catholicism?[64]

Regarding the first point, the communities of necessity dealt with the poorer sections of the population. The military government considered them actually or potentially hostile. It spied on the communities, arrested and mistreated some of the leaders, and expelled foreign priests. The Vicariate was attacked by the government as a refuge for communists and opponents, and as being linked with "terrorists." The Catholic hierarchy, including Cardinal Juan Francisco Fresno Larraín, have strongly supported the Vicariate.[65] But this did not prevent a sizable section of the clergy from favoring less social and more spiritual activity in the Base Communities; not just for theological reasons. There is fear of too much political involvement and its consequences for the church under the military dictatorship.

This view is shared by a sizeable section of wealthy Catholics. They were supporters of the military regime from the beginning. They have not hesitated to attack the clergy as being largely Marxist and as being responsible for programs threatening the public order. While the official church is, almost desperately, trying to remain politically neutral (though it has openly criticized actions of the government), these wealthier Catholics through organizations they finance (Opus Dei and others) ardently defend the government and, in the same breath, criticize the increasing politicization of their church.[66]

On the second point, what kind of Catholicism, "el popular" or the institutionalized Catholicism, no agreement was reached. Yet, from the participation of many clergymen in the rites and rituals of the popular church, their sympathy with it could be concluded. With the church under continuous attacks, harassment and distorted denunciations by the government, the clergy is preoccupied with problems of survival more than theological problems. A final answer to this question is not likely to be given as long as the military regime remains in control.

The same applies to the activities of the Liberation theologians and their followers. The government's and its Catholic supporters' hostility toward them can be taken for granted. The suppressive tactics of the government does not give them much room for expression, and even less for any concrete execution of their program. However, the election of "progressive" bishops to the positions of president and secretary general of the Chilean Bishops Conference in January 1988 might be an encouragement to the Liberation theologians. One hundred fifty of them made President Pinochet "responsible for all the atrocities we have lived through" and called him unqualified for a new term of office. In June 1988, the Bishops Conference accused the government of severely restricting the opposition during the campaign for the forthcoming plebiscite on the presidential election. The government, in turn, branded the church "an obstacle" to Chile's social order. Under these conditions, the suggestion of the new president of the Bishops Conference, of the cardinal and of the United States for a "dialogue" is not likely to be accepted by President Pinochet.[67] (In October 1988 Pinochet lost the referendum which would have allowed him to stay in power until 1997.)

In the meantime, the poor will have to endure their fate for many more years to come. The wealthy Chilean Catholics seem to be difficult subjects for conversion. The Liberation theologians have little influence and a relatively small following. And the official Chilean church will have to reconcile the various contending factions under a more liberal future government before it can gain enough support for participation in changing social structures.

This survey of the church's and theology's position in some Latin American states makes clear that the Catholic church is in motion. The movement is too young to allow a firm conclusion about the eventual results, or even only about the permanent direction further developments will take. Yet some statements can be made about the outcome the triangular controversy between the church, the theologians, and the politicians has had so far.

1. The Euro-centered character of the Catholic church has disappeared. The center of debate has shifted to Latin America. Theological creativity and religiously founded action are located in Latin America. Inevitably, Rome is involved. But Rome reacts, with the initiative coming from Latin America. The discourse there is radiating out to Rome and to the entire Third World, instead of, as formerly, the Third World receiving the waves emanating from Rome. The Catholic church is becoming universal beyond the general validity of its ethical values through having to adjust doctrine and Magisterium to historic realities everywhere.[68]

2. The questions raised in Latin America by theologians and clergy are predominantly related to the material, and therefore, spiritual conditions of the poor masses. They are forcing the church to think about its roots and its fundamental duties and mission, half forgotten in the wealthy European world. In the Third World environment it is perhaps not a betrayal of the church's evangelical message to place it at the service also of strategies for material liberation on the way to spiritual liberation and the Kingdom of Heaven. Under European conditions, with the most elementary problems of daily survival solved, the church could proceed to confront the remaining problems by theorizing about them as a first step. Under Third World conditions this procedure is an unaffordable luxury. The problems there are being lived; theorizing about them is a *cura posterior*.

3. The Latin American situation also demonstrates the luxury, if not impossibility, of neatly separating the realms of Caesar and the church. This may, at best, be a possibility at a level above concerns with daily survival. Where this level has not been reached, obtaining the minimal necessities of life does indeed become a political as well as a religious question, with both interpenetrating each other. Rome has been aware of this phenomenon since the call went out for the change of "evil social structures." The Latin American situation is highlighting the urgency of an answer and forcing the translation of rhetoric into reality. The necessity of the Latin American churches to coexist with a great variety of political regimes can serve as a valuable lesson and precedent for peoples in similar situations everywhere. Under Third World conditions, Rome's answer of the irrelevancy of governmental forms as long as they adhere to Christian values had proven inadequate, hence unacceptable to Latin Americans.

4. Finally, the Latin American situation brings to the fore the role of the people. It is certainly true that the Catholic church, as it has organized itself through the centuries, is not a democratic institution, as Joseph Cardinal Malula of Zaire said in 1985. Yet, the Latin American message is clear—as it is elsewhere—that the poor masses are asking for space within the church to participate in religious decisions and responsibilities. So indeed does the clergy in many parts of the world. The problem goes under the name of horizontalism and evokes the worst fears among the hierarchy. The dispute over the Ecclesiastic Base Communities arises in part over this problem. In countries where Catholicism is taken less seriously by Catholics, the official church can afford to let this problem linger. Latin America, where Catholicism, if not the formal church, remains very relevant, shows the need for a solution of the problem. The survival and even expansion of the communities may indicate the manner in which this need may be satisfied.

12

Pope John Paul II and Liberation Theology

The positions of Pope John Paul II and some of his predecessors on Liberation Theology, as compared to those of the Roman curia, may seem unclear. Making a distinction between the two could seem uncalled for in view of the hierarchical organization of the church. Empirical evidence, however, justifies it. The pronouncements of the Congregation for the Doctrine of the Faith, for instance, or of the *Osservatore Romano* on Liberation Theology are usually more consistent and more negative than those of the pope. Vatican officials themselves hint at the possibility of divisions of opinions carrying over into policies. An earlier pope joked, "After all, I am only the pope around here." Cardinal Ratzinger on the other hand strongly rejected such a distinction. Leonardo Boff confirmed, when attacks upon his Theology emanated from the Vatican, "We have good friends in Rome." Further evidence will suggest the possibility.

A survey of the pope's approach to Liberation Theology—and therefore to the problem of poverty—will demonstrate his qualified acquiescence, if not more. This in spite of frequent ambiguities in the pope's spoken and written messages. But these seeming uncertainties have several causes. They will clarify why these uncertainties do not necessarily reflect the pope's fairly clear and persistent fundamental position. They will also call attention to the constraints under which popes have to express their views.

On many topics, a pope's statements are sufficiently broad to lend themselves to various interpretations. He is dealing with a great variety of followers in Latin America, with a global constituency, with a diversity of governments. He must avoid confrontations, if possible. He can do this best by formulating his statements in a somewhat ambiguous fashion. He must also be cautious and, in many instances, confirmatory rather than pioneering.

The incrementally rather than radically innovative character of encyclicals is the popes' manner of adjusting to the "changing signs of the times." The unity of the Catholic church is forever uppermost in their minds. Groups of the most diverse convictions must therefore be able to reconcile themselves to cautious and not always clear-cut expressions of the church's posture. No one group can expect to find forever full approval or disapproval of its views, policies, or actions, except in regard to the most fundamental church principles.

A papal statement is frequently adjusted to time, place, and audience. Where the clergy or bishops are in conflict with secular authorities, the pope will try to match their stand, even if he does not altogether agree with it. Such practice may lead to seeming contradictions when they are more likely expedient adjustments. During the Latin American visits of Pope John Paul II in 1983 and 1985, for instance, church officials explained that no matter where the pontiff speaks, his address is directed at all Latin America but that he chooses to deal with one major topic at a time, whether the topic is particularly relevant to the country or not. He is therefore more likely to speak favorably on Liberation Theology in Brazil than in Colombia.

Occasionally, the behavior of a pope may clarify where his sympathies lie. He may not speak or shake hands with a cleric closely identified with a given viewpoint. He may avoid a visit to a particular locality. He may refuse to enter into the discussion of a certain subject.

Papal statements on the liberation of human beings on earth have enabled protagonists and opponents of Liberation Theology alike to find papal support in their respective positions. Nevertheless, there is increasing parallelism between popes and Liberation theologians on three counts. They agree on the prevailing misery of the masses in Latin America; on demands for improvements; and on the analysis of the roots of this misery.

But on the last count there can be much disagreement regarding the consequences of the analysis. Yet even on this point there is significant agreement at least on the need for changing social structures, having freer governments, providing more education, and so on. There is less agreement on how these changes are to be brought about or what they should be. But then, the pope as well as the theologians are weak on this point. Improvements can mainly be found in the less Euro-centered views of the last popes. *Sollicitudo rei socialis,* 1988, chap. III, elaborates at great length on the worldwide aspects of the poverty problem in general and development problems in particular, though it does so more in a critical vein of existing rather than the proposal of specific new practices.

In view of strong criticism of Liberation Theology as being penetrated by Marxism, repeating in summary fashion coincidences between Marxism and papal positions on the politics of poverty (already mentioned earlier) is of interest both as an illustration of the incremental development of papal positions and also eventually of John Paul II's position on the Theology.

The extensive analysis of the economic causes of poverty in papal encyclicals began, with only a few years delay, with Marx's and Engels' major writings (and had begun by theologians before that time). In the course of time, and until this day, the coincidences in analysis became ever more pronounced as, in typical fashion, one encyclical built upon its predecessor.

Leo XIII identified the laboring class as exploited by the class of the owners. Pius XI condemned the international system of free enterprise, whose "country is where profits are" as being responsible for the increasing number of "nonowning poor" whose "groans cry to God from earth." John XXIII sanctioned cooperation with communists for the achievement of limited objectives. From then on, popes and Roman Synods of Bishops made similar analyses almost routinely. Pope Paul VI and the Synods called for an end to the "scandalous" differences between the rich and the poor, and for changes in social, political, and economic systems producing them. Pope Paul VI expressed in 1974 what was by then no longer very innovative: that in proclaiming liberation and ranging itself with those working and suffering for it, the church could not allow itself to be limited to the purely religious sphere while ignoring the temporal problems of man. At the same time, however, it must reaffirm the primacy of its spiritual role, refusing to replace the proclamation of God's reign with the preaching of purely human liberations, and insisting that even its contribution to liberation would be incomplete and imperfect if it failed to preach salvation in Jesus Christ.

In the encyclical *Populorum progressio,* 1967 no. 31, (quoted earlier) revolutionary uprisings are approved under specified but unspecific conditions. "We know, however, that a revolutionary uprising—save where there is manifest, long-standing tyranny which would do great damage to fundamental personal rights and dangerous harm to the common good for the country—produces new injustices." Such a position turned out very soon to be problematic in a concrete and probably unexpected situation.

At the Fourth Bishops Synod in Rome, 1974, two Latin American bishops referred to the reality and acuteness of the problem the church had in relation to revolution and to the combination of liberation from sin with the liberation from earthly misery. They declared as unhelpful

John Paul II's formulation that the "first liberation . . . must be from sin . . . which is the cause of 'social sin' and oppressive structures." Cardinal Lorscheider of Brazil pointed out that in many Latin American states the church is asked to involve itself in a kind of, often violent, revolution as the only opportunity for evangelization. The Latin American episcopal conference, he continued, was most concerned with the manner in which the Roman Catholic church was to deal with revolutionaries, guerrillas, and guerrilla priests "who had become a source of embarrassment to the established church."[1] In discussing this issue, John Paul II, then still a cardinal, showed little sympathy for Liberation Theology. The Synod, however, backed the conscientization of the people and participation in the struggle for political, economic and social liberation.

Paul VI took up the conclusions of the Synod in his encyclical *Evangelii nuntiandi,* 1975, and spoke of "various" human liberations, anticipating John Paul II's later saying, "Theology of Liberation, yes, but which one?" Both popes remained ambiguous, but not unfavorably so to the Theology. This ambiguity continued when John Paul II gave speeches at the Puebla Conference in 1979, enabling those favoring and those opposing the Theology to take some encouragement for their views.

Conservatives felt comforted by the pope's reminder that the Puebla Conference[2] must not disregard "the incorrect interpretations" that have sometimes resulted in regard to the Medellín conclusions which call for "calm discernment, opportune criticism, and clear-cut stances." They also found comforting the pope's telling priests and religious that they were not "social directors, political leaders, or functionaries of a temporal power." Their primary task was to cultivate "a union with God through a profound interior life." He rejected a portrait of Christ "as a political activist, as a fighter against Roman domination and the authorities, and even as someone involved in the class struggle. This conception of Christ as a political figure, a revolutionary, a subversive from Nazareth, did not tally with the church's catechesis because it confuses the claims of Jesus' accusers with the attitudes of Jesus himself; because it was ignoring the Lord's willing self-surrender or even his awareness of his redemptive mission." Conservatives could take comfort, finally, from the pope's questioning the propriety of setting up a People's church, "one which is 'born of the people' and is fleshed out in the poor" and, as he added later, which is "not of Christ."

The pope had something to say to comfort Liberation theologians as well. He stressed that the church must serve the poor, the needy, and the marginalized. Human beings were not pawns of political and economic processes and must participate in decisions affecting them. There was a "social mortgage" on all private property obliging their owners to use it for the common good. Reforms were needed to implement these principles. The reformers could take even more comfort from the pope's speech to the Indians in the states of Oxaca and Chiapas—a speech which he sharpened in the night before its delivery[3]—in which he emphasized the more temporal aspects of his opening address: The Indians had a right to human dignity, to freedom from oppression, to decent wages, to the beneficial consequences of the "social mortgage" on private property, and to early reforms for the improvement of their lives here and now.[4] (In late 1986, he talked similarly to the Australian aborigines.)

A few days after his return from Mexico, the pope said, "Frequently, the impression is created that the Liberation Theology . . . is related to Latin America. Against this impression one has to agree with one of the great contemporary theologians who demands a Liberation theology of universal dimensions." (The late Urs von Balthasar had said in 1985, "One must change some things and one must not turn it into a drama. There is the great hope that the intuition of St. Francis of Assisi may continue in a theology, a theology of 'liberation.' You know, the word 'liberation' is in the Gospel, the poor are in there too!"). But doubts have been raised whether a universally valid Liberation Theology can exist.[5]

The publication of the encyclical *Laborem exercens* in 1981 (no. 12) was an important indicator of the pope's clearly "leaning to the left." The encyclical's main subject was the dignity of the worker. It delved deeply into the degradation of the workers resulting from the identification of the worker with the instruments of production, leading to "proletarian-ization" and the dichotomy between capital and labor. By contrast, it pointed out, the church had always taught *"the principle of the priority of labor over capital."* The church must therefore give prominence to the primacy of man over things and the prevention of proletarianization. To achieve social justice, ever new movements are needed to achieve solidarity of and with the workers. Such solidarity must exist "whenever it is called for by the social degrading of the subject of work, by exploitation of workers, and by the growing areas of poverty and even hunger. The Church is firmly committed to this cause, for she considers it her mission, her service, a proof of her fidelity to Christ, so that she can truly be the 'Church of the poor.' "

The terminology in this encyclical and much of its social analysis was reminiscent of Marxism. This is not to say that it followed Marxism any more than would be true of many Liberation theologians. It did, how-ever, bring the standpoints of the pope and the Liberation theologians closer together. The pope's visit to Central America in 1983 was there-fore expected with great interest by the reform-minded section of the church there.

But this visit, instead of providing further clarification of the pope's stand on matters of the poor and what to do about them in the spirit of *Laborem exercens*, 1981, turned out to be, in the words of the *National*

Catholic Review reporter, a "pilgrimage of contradictions," and a disappointment to adherents of Liberation Theology.

The pope said so many different things to so many different people that once again all parties to the controversy could pick out something to support their positions. It was reasonably clear, though, and perhaps reflected the Vatican's more than the pope's stance that, as an observer put it, in El Salvador and Nicaragua the pope played "Washington's game," which was, of course, also playing the local official church's game.[6]

The pope abandoned evenhandedness. He was sharply critical of the Nicaraguan government, though not without some clumsy provocation by that government. He carefully avoided antagonizing the Salvadoran government. He chastised Nicaragua but failed to condemn El Salvador for their violations of human rights. He had much good to say about the Salvadoran government and nothing bad. He had much bad to say about the Nicaraguan government and nothing good. Disregarding his own admonition that every person deserves respect as a human being, he refused to let the priests and religious serving in the Nicaraguan government share in communion and ostentatiously refused to shake hands with them. In El Salvador, he praised the men and women killed in the service to Christ. In Nicaragua, where nobody has been killed in the service to Christ under the Sandinista government, he refused to bless 17 young men who had been killed in the anti-Somoza struggle, calling their mothers' request for a blessing an insult.[7]

Nowhere did the pope visit slums or refugee camps, although some 12,000 Salvadoran refugees in a camp in Honduras were eagerly waiting for his visit. In Nicaragua, he had no words of consolation or inspiration. He made no reference to the people's effort at self-improvement. He neither criticized the Somoza regime nor praised the Sandinista revolution. He talked mostly of the church's authority and warned against constructing institutions challenging this authority—an unmistakable criticism of the Base Communities and the People's church. In most other countries he visited, he again pleaded for the poor and oppressed, condemned methods of totalitarianism, and called for changes in political, economic, and social systems.

In spite of the pope's reserve regarding Liberation Theology, some faction in the Vatican was reported as worried that the pope's exposure to the living conditions of Central American peasants and the oppressive ruthlessness of some governments had "softened" him on Liberation Theology. Their anxiety was augmented when they found out that the pope changed some of his speeches prepared by Cardinal Baggio, president of the Pontifical Mission for Latin America, to show greater compassion with the poor, and less criticism of Liberation Theology.

The pope's next visit to South America in February 1985 provided only a bit more clarity about his thought on Liberation Theology. Initially, his statements were disappointing. The *New York Times*[8] reporter described the pope's messages as jumping back and forth between consolation of the poor and calls for greater church discipline, respect for church authority, and the avoidance of wrong doctrines. He appeared pre-occupied by fears of a parallel church when he told priests and nuns to shun all ideas of a "double hierarchy or double magisterium" and to remain firm on orthodoxy.

The reporter for the *National Catholic Review* complained that during the pope's first stop in Venezuela, he had no nod to the poor, no word on Venezuela's crushing economic problems, no criticism on machismo. Business leaders, he wrote, were exploiting the visit as "Alka Seltzer" for the poor and the government was wasting great resources for the pope's reception.[9] But as the visit proceeded, the tenor of the pope's messages changed, even while he was still in Venezuela. He commiserated with the poor, called for structural changes in the economic system, improvements in human rights, but also warned the clergy against becoming involved in politics.

In other countries, his speeches became more "radical." In Peru and Ecuador, he rejected, as always and everywhere, recourse to violence or "ideologies" as solutions to social problems. He called for just wages, land reforms, social security, stronger labor unions. He scorned the international system, especially the stringent conditions imposed by the International Monetary Fund. Ignoring government suggestions, he visited slums and Indian settlements in Peru. In the first, he praised the work of the Base Communities, encouraging them to continue their good work. He appealed to them to fight for better living conditions and to discard machismo. Yet he preceded his remarks by suggesting caution in reinterpreting the Bible as "inspiring political visions," and by con-demning the "falsities and false prophets, the rereading of the Gospel in non-ecclesiastical terms inspired by social and political vision." To the Indians he talked in their own language, castigating their exploitation and strongly supporting their land claims.[10] Occasional barbs against Liberation Theology during his tour were presumably too subtle to be understood by the large and enthusiastic crowds meeting him along the way.

Many listeners to the pope's speeches were mystified, once more, by the seeming contradictions and by some of his behavior. But to some extent, these could be explained by the constraints upon popes in expressing their views. Members of his delegation attempted to clarify his remarks. His views were colored, they said, by Rome's preoccupation with the Nicaraguan situation and concern over a possible schism there.

Condemnation of the People's church in Nicaragua should not be taken as criticism of the Ecclesiastic Base Communities in other countries.[11]

In February, 1988, John Paul II published his massive encyclical *Sollicitudo rei socialis* on the social doctrine of the church. The statement was sweeping and general, and essentially a summary of what Pope John Paul II and his predecessors had said about the social concerns of the church, but brought up to date in the light of contemporary conditions. In weighing the positive against the negative aspects of the situation today, the encyclical found a distressing overweight in the negative factors. It proceeded to analyze and enumerate them without adding much to previous encyclicals.

The plague on both houses, the capitalist and the communist, was repeated. Their rivalry was made responsible for delaying human progress. Neither was found "capable of changes and updatings such as to favor or promote a true and integral development of individuals and peoples in modern societies." Yet, the integral human development is the church's main concern. Its achievement is not only a matter of material improvements. Poverty was defined as the deprivation of worldly goods and human rights. Only a development satisfying both requirements was true "development on the human level." The church "does not have *technical solutions to offer*" to bring about such a development. Nor is the church's a third position between Marxism and capitalism or between any other less radically opposed alternatives. The church's role is to watch that however the "structures of sin" are altered and the "long and complex" path to integral human development is trodden, human dignity was preserved and moral values were dominant.

The church's contribution to such development was conversion, and guidance toward the higher value of social solidarity; meaning commitment to the common good and responsibility of all for all. The rich must feel responsible for the poor and share with them "all they possess." The poor "in the same spirit of solidarity" should be neither passive nor destructive of the social fabric but do all they too can do for the common good. The "intermediate" groups should not selfishly insist upon their own interests but respect the interests of others. What applies to individuals within national societies of all in the Third or Fourth Worlds should apply to states in the international society as well. Only by way of example were a few needed measures "inspired by solidarity and love of preference for the poor" enumerated.

Turning to Liberation Theology as a way to promote human development, the encyclical referred to "a new way of confronting the problems of poverty and underdevelopment" recently spread in some areas of the world, especially in Latin America. This approach makes liberation "the fundamental category and the first principle of action." The encyclical conceded "positive values" to this way, but also pointed out the possibility of deviations and the risks of deviations "damaging to the faith" connected with this form of theological reflection and method. However, the aspiration to freedom from all forms of slavery affecting the individual and society was recognized as,"noble and legitimate." "This in fact is the purpose of development, or rather liberation and development, taking into account the intimate connection between the two." But, the encyclical repeated, development and liberation, to be authentic, must go beyond economic and include cultural, transcendent and religious elements. If it does, the church "must affirm her confidence in a *true liberation.*"

In spite of the inconclusive messages and actions of Pope John Paul II, some tentative conclusions regarding his position on Liberation Theology might be drawn.

1. The pope objects strongly to political activities or their advocacy by Liberation theologians. How his demands for changes in the sinful structures or structures of sin might be brought about—other than by conversion—and by what kind of structures they are to be replaced, he leaves unanswered. His unqualified plague on both houses attitude appears to demonstrate how strongly he insists upon political neutrality, presumably to preserve the church's international influence. It could well be that the pope's contingent identification of the theologians with Marxists leads him to oppose their political activity more than activity per se. Father Giuseppe Brunelli in Maputo, Mozambique, was probably close to the truth when he said about his own political activity, "But the church has always been in politics. Only, the Nicaraguan priests are in politics that the church does not agree with, so it opposes them. If I were in the traditional conservative line, there would be no problem."[12]

2. There is consistency in the pope's rejection of the use of violence for any purpose. Pitting humans against humans denies Christian insistence on brotherly love and conversion to produce solidarity as the major foundation for social action. Yet even here, the church has made exceptions. The use of violence is not condemned under all circumstances. There can be disagreement only whether the stringent conditions permitting the use of violence are fulfilled. The pope does not think they are in Latin America. But there is no disagreement with most Liberation theologians on this point.

3. The pope is extremely anxious about the danger of a parallel church arising from Liberation Theology and the Base Communities. His fears may be somewhat assuaged by a better understanding now of "el popular," the popular church in contradistinction to a People's church. Nevertheless, denials by Liberation theologians of the rise of a parallel church notwithstanding, the nationalism coloring Libera-

tion Theology is creating some gulf of uncertain depth between the Latin American church and Rome. Conciliatory statements and actions emanating from the pope will help to bridge it. In the meantime, the pope's frequent emphasis on the divinely instituted primacy and hierarchical organization of the Roman Catholic church is presumably a warning against any deviations in this respect.

4. This emphasis may be motivated by more than the wish to preserve orthodoxy, some Latin American clergy are speculating. The pope may aim at securing his preeminent position so that he can more successfully lead the church to a new "Christian civilization" he has mentioned on several occasions; or to introduce his own Liberation Theology, which he is said to plan. Some Latin American clerics explained: The pope is all in favor of material liberation in addition to spiritual liberation, but it must be achieved in his way. His elaborations of liberation in *Sollicitudo rei socialis,* 1988, deal favorably with themes dear to Liberation theologians. The spirit of both *Instructions* is unrecognizable in the encyclical. His differences with the Liberation Theologians have certainly diminished over the years.

5. There can be no doubt about the pope's great concern with the prevailing injustices, poverty and dehumanization of life through either capitalism or communism. Hence his advocacy of change in the man-made social structures responsible for these evils, though in what direction specifically he left unclear, except that new structures must reflect Christian values. His constant emphasis upon solidarity and community indicates the trend in which he wants society to move. The end result is reminiscent of precapitalist times, and it might ameliorate class differences. It would also be a Christian solution in the sense of embracing all humankind, whatever an individual's economic status. It is more a moral than a sociological solution, making its otherwise patent anachronism less relevant. By advocating it, the pope's position becomes highly idealistic, but avoids the risk of coming yet closer to Marxism. Some Liberation theologians have gone a step further by accepting the possibility of a democratic socialism. If pressed to detail future structures, would Pope John Paul II accept something resembling a democratic or humanitarian socialism? If his—and some of his predecessors—neutrality on the nature of any system as long as it embodies Christian values were to be taken at face value, the answer should be yes. It should also be yes if the consequences of the pope's criticisms of prevailing systems and his hints at what needs to be done, were to become reality. But this would inevitably involve some elements of Marxism, unacceptable to pope and Vatican—when called by that name.

Some Liberation theologians argue their criticism by the pope as Marxists is a misinterpretation of their position. Leonardo Boff once said that the theologians did not recognize themselves in their description by Rome. Marxism, most claim, is useful to them as a method of social analysis, not as a system to serve their Christian purposes. They are not any more influenced by Marxism than the popes when they write their social encyclicals, they maintain. When church officials explain that the apparent influence of Marxism in the encyclicals is not equivalent to taking over Marxism as a self-contained entity, the theologians answer that their situation is not any different. They also claim that nowadays social analysis without recourse or resemblance to Marxist analysis is impossible.

Hans-Peter Kalvenbach, superior-general of the Jesuits, emphasized, in speaking approvingly of Liberation Theology, that Latin American Marxism is not monolithic.[13] Marxist terminology, when applied to social systems, is necessary, but its meaning was quite different from the way Marxism is manifested "in existing Marxist systems." In a similar vein, Gutiérrez, in justifying his own use of Marxist terminology and analysis, contended that just as one cannot talk about modern psychology without reference to Freudian ideas without being a Freudian, so one has to refer to Marx in social matters without having to accept Marxism.[14] Differences between themselves and Pope John Paul II, Liberation theologians say, are not due to a denial on their part of the essentials of Catholicism but mainly to the failure of the "European" Catholics to understand the homegrown Third World interpretation of Catholicism. This failure may pass as the pope's views become more truly universal. His frequent travels to the Third World are exposing him to the reality of poverty. His latest encyclical is said to have been composed after consultation with bishops conferences all over the world. And a comparison of his speech in Lima, Peru, in 1985, when he warned against "passing ideologies," and his speeches in Latin America in 1988 when he called for reconciliation between "right and left" and regional self-help shows the trend of his views toward Liberation Theology.

Unfortunately for reconciliation, the pope is surrounding himself with, and appointing to Latin America, individuals less liberal than he is on Liberation Theology. Cardinal Ratzinger and some other high officials, the *National Catholic Reporter* stated, stand well to the right of the pope.[15] They have no inhibitions in using their influence against the growth of the Theology and they have had some success, in spite of Boff speaking of the pope as an "ally." There may be some ecclesiastic-political consideration or some wishful thinking affecting Boff's characterization. But without doubt some conflictful situations have arisen within the Vatican over the Theology. To what extent Liberation Theology and the poor will be affected depends upon the outcome of this conflict.

13
The Vatican and Liberation Theology

In the early years of Liberation Theology little was publicly heard from the Vatican. The liberalism of Vatican II was still influencing the church. The stress was on collegiality, dialogue, participation, and so on. This spirit was reflected in Pope Paul VI's apostolic exhortation *Evangelii nuntiandi,* 1975, to more and more Christians to devote themselves to the liberation of man. The church would provide these Christians with faith and fraternal love. These were to be the foundation of their wisdom and experience when engaging in a liberation effort and translating them into forms of action, participation, and commitment. But opposition to the theology came almost at once after its birth from clergy, theologians, and laymen, Latin Americans included.

Prominent among these last were (and are) Alphonso Lopez Trujillo and Father Roger Vekemans, both with good relations to the Vatican. They were strongly supported by conservatives, especially the German organization Adveniat (and also the United States, Opus Dei, and others). Adveniat in particular had been founded in Germany in 1961 for the purpose of helping the Latin American church, mainly in Brazil and Ecuador. For 1987, for instance, it planned 2247 projects for a total of DM.44.3 million. It finances the convening of conferences, recruiting and training of priests, publishing studies, and especially media of all kinds.[1]

In 1973, the chairman of the Episcopal Commission Adveniat, Bishop F. Hengsbach, during a visit to Latin America, established the Study Group Church and Liberation (Studienkreis Kirche and Befreiung), headquartered in Germany and devoted to the opposition of Liberation Theology. Its German members, among them L. Bossle, Professor A. Rauscher and W. Weber, were not without opposition from other Germans. This became evident when a statement "Memorandum of West German Theologians on the Campaign against the Theology of Liberation 1977" appeared, signed by N. Greinacher, J. B. Metz, the late Karl Rahner, and others.[2] But it did not stop the conservatives' or their Latin American friends' activities against Liberation Theology several years before the Vatican began to take public stands.

The Vatican apparently decided toward the end of the 1970s to participate actively and publicly in putting a brake on Liberation Theology's progress. The decision coincided with that of Pope John Paul II to give the Catholic church a stronger presence and profile in the world. This goal, the pope seemed to feel, required unity in the church, best guaranteed by strong centralization based upon a strict hierarchical order. Because Vatican officials conceived of Liberation Theology and the Ecclesiastic Base Communities as a threat to both, they began to take measures, perhaps more enthusiastically than the pope wished, against the theology.

The major burden of this task fell upon Joseph Cardinal Ratzinger and Sebastiano Cardinal Baggio, president of the Pontifical Mission for Latin America and later prefect of the Political Commission. A major channel of communication with Latin America was Cardinal Trujillo and his close collaborator, Roger Vekemans. Cardinal Trujillo's influence rested on his positions as secretary general of CELAM 1972-1979, then president 1980-1983. The Vatican had, in addition, the normal contacts with Latin American bishops, priests, nuns, and nuncios, but they were reported to be less regular.

Cardinal Trujillo is by now (he was not always) an enthusiastic conservative in the Catholic church. He achieved a meteoric career from an unknown clergyman in Colombia to Cardinal in Bogotá. His brilliance, cleverness, political acumen, and outspokenness got him his position in the hierarchy, but also made him a feared man to his opponents. He has been called the "most feared and powerful" man in Latin America. Many people give him credit for his untiring efforts to prevent Marxist penetration of the Catholic church. They believe it is unfair to paint him as an "archvillain" as some other people do.[3]

The cardinal's campaign against Liberation Theology began in 1972 and has proceeded forcefully ever since. Among his favorite targets were the Christians for Socialism and the Latin American Confederation of Religions (CLAR), a standard-bearer of Liberation Theology. His position is clear and simple. The Theology is a communist doctrine. Its protagonists and followers are attempting to infiltrate and subvert the church. They are either Marxists or naive victims of Marxists. They must be fought and he is doing so with great devotion.

He is not choosy in his strategies, tactics, and methods. They range from pamphleteering to public accusations and political maneuvering. His manner was demonstrated, for instance, in his not altogether unsuccessful manipulation of membership, committee composition, and working papers at the Puebla Conference with a view to having it retreat from some of the forward positions of Medellín; or in his attacks on *Pax Christi* whose document at Puebla he dubbed "openly unjust, hostile to the hierarchy," and lacking objectivity.[4]

Father Roger Vekemans, with an interesting and checkered career behind him, is a more suave person, which does not prevent him from violently attacking Liberation Theology. He is also an expert on Europe and North America, where he apparently has access to large financial resources for his fight against the Theology.

Cardinal Ratzinger at the time of Vatican II thought the church would make a grave mistake to isolate itself "in the shabby ghetto of orthodoxy." Since then, he has become the foremost defender of what is considered a "restoration" of the church away from Vatican II and toward orthodox traditionalism. He is convinced Vatican II initiated "a progressive process of decadence" in the church.[5] The balance sheet of 20 years of Vatican II shows, according to him, the unleashing of "hidden, aggressive, polemic, divisive forces." A "radical liberal ideology of an individualistic, rationalistic, and hedonistic character" had penetrated the church. A "restoration to find a new balance after all these exaggerations" was necessary. Presumably a reference to the task he expected the extraordinary Synod of Bishops in November 1985 to undertake. In the eyes of the liberal clergy and theologians, Cardinal Ratzinger has become the symbol of reaction in the Vatican. They make him responsible for the many measures the church has taken during the last few years to undo the progressivism (to them) of Vatican II.

The controversy between Vatican and Liberation theologians came to a head in 1984 and 1985. By that time, much of the debate had descended somewhat from a high theological level to the oversimplified and also symbolic issue of the relation between Marxism and Catholicism. Two major events in the middle 1980s highlighted the hardening of the Vatican's stand against Liberation Theology.

The first event was the publication of *Instruction on Certain Aspects of the "Theology of Liberation"* in August 1984. The document was issued by the Congregation for the Doctrine of the Faith, signed by Cardinal Ratzinger as prefect, "and approved at an audience granted the undersigned Cardinal Prefect by His Holiness Pope John Paul II, who ordered it published." Lest the papal approval should appear as an identification of the pope with the cardinal's position, Leonardo Boff stated "The signature of the pope under such a document is a formality. It says little about his personal opinion. I even suspect that the pope distances himself from this paper."[6]

The publication had been preceded by the attendance of Cardinal Ratzinger of a meeting of the Doctrinal Commissions of Latin America in March. While there, he had discussed the themes of Liberation Theology and the People's church. Foreshadowing what was to be said in the *Instruction,* he said at a press conference upon his return to Rome that the Theology had diverse expressions: some fully legitimate, some subject to criticism, some unacceptable. "In this regard critical reflection is indispensable, beginning with the liberating dimension of the Christian faith. Faith is liberating, but provided it remains authentic faith, without letting it be contaminated by foreign elements."[7] With the presentation of the *Instruction,* wrote the *Osservatore Romano,* "critical reflection" had arrived and was now in everyone's reach.

Bishop Quarrancio of Argentina presented the document to the press. He supplied some comments which—intentionally or unintentionally— set the tone for much of the comment to come and perhaps intended to soften the shock the document was expected to produce in some church circles.

The document, he admitted, was certainly critical within the sphere which it intended to confront, but nevertheless it was not basically negative. "In fact, it not only admits the *possibility* of a theological reflection on the subject of liberation but also recognizes the 'spiritual and practical wealth' of it. In addition, it recognizes the validity of the expression 'liberation theology' and of the underlying theological discourse, as long as it is well understood." Cardinal Ratzinger amplified the document was meant to be "a contribution to the elimination of all the obstacles which up to the present have slowed the process of evangelization and of an authentic and total liberation" in Latin America.[8]

The *Instruction,* Introduction, IV-15, VI-4, XI-5, 8, 15, bemoaned the condition of the poor everywhere and the lack of equity in the world. The search for justice had led into the trap of wrong ideologies. Misery was the result of sin. Therefore, to advocate social reforms before the elimination of sin, was proceeding in the wrong order. It was only by making an appeal to the moral potential of the person and to the constant need for interior conversion, that social change would be brought about which would be truly in the service of man. Certain forms of Liberation Theology must be condemned because they used "in an insufficiently critical manner, concepts borrowed from various currents of marxist thought." This condemnation was not "a disavowel of all those who want to respond generously and with an authentic evangelical spirit to the 'preferential option for the poor.' " Rather, it related to the reduction of liberation in the Theology to a principally or exclusively political or economic enterprise. This amounted to an impermissible reduction of the Gospel to a "purely earthly gospel." The poor of the scripture are not the poor of Marx's proletariat. This confusion also applied to the People's church and the Base Communities. They betray the goodwill of the members who ignore the falsification because they "lack the necessary catechical and theological preparation as well as the discernment to recognize the falseness of theses popularized by the theologies of liberation."

An examination of Marxism led the *Instruction* to declare it totally incompatible with Christianity. Any useful analysis in Marxism or any other philosophy must undergo a critical study from the theological perspective before it could be used for its instrumental value. In the struggle for truth and justice the church wants to come to the aid of the poor not through Marxism but "in the light of the Beatitudes and especially the Beatitude of the poor at heart." Liberation was achieved not through class struggle but by "freeing oneself from a delusion in order to base oneself squarely on the Gospel and its power of realization." Liberation Theology, the People's church and the Ecclesiastic Base Communities were found contrary to the teachings of the Catholic church mainly because they were oriented toward the here and now and because they challenged the sacramental and hierarchical structure of the church.

Different people could interpret the *Instruction* in different ways. Cardinal Ratzinger was pleased because, he hinted, if everybody could feel to be the target, the warning of the document to all was successful.[9] What was beyond doubt was that the statement had very little to say on how the poor might be helped and justice might be established—which, after all, is the goal of Liberation Theology.

The pope was described as "surprised and perplexed" by the sharp criticism of the *Instruction* coming from many sides.[10] The promise in the *Instruction* that it would be followed by another, more "positive" document on Liberation Theology was presumably due to the pope's intervention, but had little mollifying effect—nor did the introduction to the *Instruction*, reportedly suggested by the pope, acknowledging the existence of great misery in Latin America which was responsible for the rise of Liberation Theology in the first place. Perhaps in yet another attempt by the pope to defuse the *Instruction*'s explosive effect was his speech in Edmonton, Canada, two weeks after the document's publication, in which he stressed the need to aid the poor. He decried the exclusive individualistic interpretation of the Christian ethic, insisting that it also had a "social dimension." Christians were obliged to change the "rigid structures" in societies, impeding peace, development, and human rights. He supported the Third World's demand for the redistribution of wealth, now amassed in the First World by the "imperialistic monopoly of economic and political supremacy at the expense of others."[11] Pope John Paul II showed no public reaction to the *Instruction*. He used his influence to soften its impact from which the conclusion is permitted that he did not share the ferocity of its tenor.

Most Liberation theologians reacted calmly. They felt the pronouncement had built up a strawman. They were not the individuals Cardinal Ratzinger had in mind. Boff said, the theologians did not recognize themselves in the descriptions. Gutiérrez said, what the cardinal described was not his "itinerary."[12] Brazilian Cardinal Ivo Lorscheiter thought the initial consternation produced by the document had faded after "the progressives" announced that their work would not be hindered by Rome's "rap on the knuckles."

Initial responses to the *Instruction* were cautious. Most Latin American bishops suggested to the clergy careful study of the document and avoidance of panic. As the meaning of the document continued to be examined, reactions became more pronounced and antithetical. But nobody seemed to change positions. On the contrary, many people feared a sharpening of a division in the Latin American church. The bishops favoring Liberation Theology attempted to highlight the more "positive" aspects of the *Instruction*. They rejected the reproach of Marxist influence. The Theology was not derived from Marxism but from living among the poor. That was "where Liberation Theology was born. From listening to the word of God and seeing the realities lived by the poor. . . ." In answer, Eugenio Cardinal de Araujo Sales of Rio de Janeiro wrote "The battle flag raised against misery and oppression is primarily ours, and not of 'liberation theologians.' "[13]

In other parts of the world, apparently mostly those people critical of the *Instruction* expressed opinions. Many pointed out that using Marxist methodology was not equivalent to accepting Marxism. Most felt that Cardinal Ratzinger wanted to warn against the direction Liberation Theology was taking, not condemn the Theology. Their intention was apparent not to permit disagreement with the statement to be interpreted as opposition to the Vatican.[14]

A major defense of the *Instruction* as a condemnation of Liberation Theology came in the middle of 1985. Twenty-four priests, laypersons, philosophers, theologians, and sociologists from Latin America and Western Europe (among them Cardinal Trujillo, Archbishop Vargas, and Professor Rauscher) met in Chile to discuss Liberation Theology. A major question the meeting addressed was whether the statement was critical only of hypothetical positions or directed against essential conceptions of the Liberation theologians. In this manner, the participants wanted to answer those many commentators who proposed that either the statement referred to nonessential parts of the Theology or was a warning against possible future development rather than a disapprobation of the Theology in its contemporary form.

In a long "Declaration of the Andes"[15] the members of the meeting concluded that the statement was directed expressly against Liberation Theology. The social analysis of the Theology, the "Declaration" maintained, was based upon Marxism. The Theology incorporated uncritically Marxist and neo-Marxist ideas into theological thinking. Liberation Theology was incompatible with faith, tradition, and social teachings of the church. In a number of individual papers contributed by members of the meeting, the falseness of the Theology and the adequacy of the church's social teaching, also for the Latin American situation, were elaborated in great detail. The authors expressed the hope of contributing to the further growth of criticism which they saw developing in Latin America.

The authors were correct in visualizing a growing critique, but it came more from the United States and Europe than from Latin America (e.g. Michael Novak, Jean Kirkpatrick, Richard Rubenstein, James Schall, Malachi Martin, Jean Galot, Studienkreis Kirche and Befreiung, François H. Lepargneur, and others).

The second great event indicative of the hardening attitude in the Vatican was the silencing of Leonardo Boff on May 1, 1985. It did not arrive as a total surprise. The brief history leading up to the case indicated that it had to do as much with ecclesiastic politics as with theology.

In 1982, Cardinal Sales created in Rio de Janeiro the Archdiocesan Commission for the Doctrine of the Faith under the direction of Auxiliary Bishop Karl Josef Romer, both persons well known as opponents of Liberation Theology. The Commission's first enterprise was an attack on Leonardo Boff's book *Church: Charisma and Power*. In essence, the book did not deal with theology but with the church's abuse of its power. Boff defended himself in an article, whereupon several tradition-minded theologians entered into a debate with him.

On May 15, 1984, Cardinal Ratzinger, in the name of his Congregation, sent Boff a six-page letter, very critical of Boff's position. Boff was invited to come to Rome for a conversation with the Cardinal.[16] He was also informed that "In view of the influence the book has had on the faithful" the cardinal's letter would be published. When the pope heard of this intention, and found out that the subject had never been discussed, he forbade the publication until after a colloquium with Boff had taken place in Rome. Boff was also informed that his work was "dangerous to the faith of the whole ecclesiastical community," therefore had international significance, and had to be discussed in Rome, not in Brazil. Boff requested a clarification of the nature of the "conversation," was it to be a judicial proceeding or an informal exchange? The conversation, he was informed, was to be an informal conversation. But just before it took place, it turned out to be not judicial but official, according to prescribed rules. Only an Argentinian theologian would be present, to take notes. The official name of the conversation was "a colloquium."

The Vatican was trying to avoid giving the meeting the appearance of an inquisition, though this is what the headlines in a number of newspapers called it, and not entirely without justification. *Die Zeit,* for instance, wrote "The old Inquisition is dead. Long live the new one!"[17] The meeting was to be formal. Only Cardinal Ratzinger and the Argentinian were to be present. But Brazilian Archbishop Ivo Lorscheiter and Aloisio Cardinal Lorscheider had arrived a few days before Boff in Rome, and Cardinal Arns arrived on the day of the meeting. These prelates requested permission to be present during the colloquium which was eventually granted, not by Cardinal Ratzinger but by Cardinal Casaroli, the Vatican's Secretary of State. A compromise was reached. At first, Ratzinger and Boff would have a session, then the Brazilian prelates would join them. The meeting was to be, after all, a conversation.[18]

The conversation took place, lasting two hours. Then Cardinals Lorscheider and Arns, together with the Secretary of the Congregation for the Doctrine of the Faith joined them. During this conversation, Cardinal Arns suggested some of the methods and details for a second *Instruction* foreshadowed in the 1984 *Instruction,* which Cardinal Ratzinger accepted.

The affair attracted worldwide attention, much of it unfavorable to the Vatican. Those favoring Liberation Theology were joined by those fearing an attempt by the Vatican to cut back the liberalization following Vatican II. "I have the impression," said a European Jesuit, "that the higher officials in Rome cannot sleep anymore as soon as somewhere people thinking and acting for themselves appear. They are ignoring in principle modern problems of our culture. They can understand the unity of the Church only when it is formed by their own—European—experience. Questioning is understood as threatening." The Brazilian Bishop Adriano Hypolito asserted that the procedure would please the Brazilian conservatives and military. The brief against Boff stemmed from the perspective of dogmatists and bureaucrats unable to comprehend Latin American reality. That sociology and a "godless ideology like marxism" could make a contribution to Liberation Theology could surprise only those who were ignorant of the past alliance between church and elites and the contemporary social and economic conditions in Latin America.[19]

The mission center of the Franciscan Order in Bonn—Boff's Order—in a statement of August, 1984, sympathized fully with Boff.[20] The process was not only against him but against Liberation Theology and the millions of its adherents. Ultimately, the question was whether in the Third World the oligarchies or the poor should have the upper hand. This statement expressed a widespread opinion that the process was symbolic for the Vatican's concern over the diminution of its power expected to follow from such liberalisms as freedom of expression, horizontalism, civil rights also within the church, and more religious functions for laypersons. Not Boff's theology but his criticism of the church's structure was the issue, said a Zürich newspaper.

The Boff case did not end here. In March, 1985, the Vatican published a ten-page report—approved by the Pope—declaring Boff's criticisms unsustainable and answering them point by point. Boff declared his pleasure that Liberation Theology was not attacked and confirmed that he would continue to recognize the authority of the church—where legitimately exercised. This report was the prelude to the severest measure the Vatican had taken hitherto—and since—against Liberation Theology.

In March, 1985, Boff received a "notification," the mildest form of censure, from the Congregation for the Doctrine of the Faith and the Congregation for Religious and Secular Institutions, declaring his views "of such a nature as to imperil the sound doctrine of the Church." This notification was followed, under the date of April 26, 1985, by the imposition of three disciplinary measures upon Boff: a period of silence long enough to permit Boff "adequate reflection" and suspending any public activity; renunciation of his position on the editorial staff of a religious Brazilian journal; and submission to censorship before publication of any theological writing. Father General Vaughn of the Franciscan Order specified the length of silence as one year. Before it was ended, Boff received permission from the Vatican to publish a book arguing that priests should help the poor fight landowners, industrialists, and their oppressive governments. The ban on public activities was ended prematurely on March 1985.

Boff accepted the censure in a "religious spirit." But the rest of the interested world did not. An avalanche of protests and expressions of sympathy with Boff followed the announcement of the penalty. They came from religious and civilian circles and focused on the totalitarian method of the Vatican, on the danger of a split within the church, and on Liberation Theology. A smaller number of comments approved of the Vatican's action.

In June, 1985, Cardinal Lorscheider conversed with Pope John Paul II, complaining about the manner in which the case was handled and expressing astonishment that such usages still prevailed. They arranged a meeting between the Congregation for the Doctrine of the Faith and the Brazilian Bishops Conference, at which future proceedings were agreed to prevent the repetition of such incidents. There was also the important agreement that a new document would be published emphasizing the positive aspects of Liberation Theology, to clarify that the Boff case was not tantamount to a judgment on the Theology.

What conclusion can be drawn from the Boff case? There was certainly no contribution to any solution of the poverty problem, directly or indirectly. This vital issue was bypassed in favor of internal church politics. Once again, the effort expended by the official church on ecclesiastics, as far as the public could judge, exceeded that expended on solving problems concerning social issues—which, after all, is the central concern of Liberation Theology. Specifically regarding the Boff case, the Vatican's contention was probably correct that it related to the order and power of the hierarchy, not to Liberation Theology.[21] On that question, Pope John Paul II and Vatican were in agreement. But Boff's place in the Liberation Theology controversy made inevitable that the public would assume the Vatican's attack on Boff to have been triggered as much by his role in the development of Liberation Theology as by his criticism of the hierarchical order. The Congregation for the Doctrine of the Faith had no problem since it was opposed to both. Pope John Paul II was in a dilemma. He obviously agreed with the Congregation on the hierarchical order of the church. But he had sympathies for Liberation Theology. His mitigating position in the Boff case was presumably a way of manifesting his differences with Cardinal Ratzinger.

There were other signs during this period of a hardening in the Vatican's attitude toward "liberalism" in the Catholic church. Occasionally, Pope John Paul II shared the views of others on this point, even when it involved aspects of Liberation Theology. There seemed to be contradictions between his frequent praise for parts of Liberation Theology and the Ecclesiastic Base Communities and his support for measures restraining progressivism in the church. But these contradictions dissolve themselves when the pope's strong concern for the unity of the church and her centralization of power in Rome is remembered.

During his travels abroad, the pope seized many opportunities to warn that "the value of the great Catholic unity" might be forgotten, for instance, in creating a People's church or ecumenical communities in Africa and other parts of the world. Two "liberal" U.S. archbishops, Walter R. Sullivan of Richmond and Raymond G. Hunthausen of Seattle received "apostolic visitations" from two other American archbishops, following complaints from their communities about too much "liberalism." Hunthausen was warned and a conservative auxiliary bishop was attached to his office. Father Charles Curran was relieved of his teaching position in 1986 at the Catholic University of America because of his liberal stand on birth control and other issues. Some academics favoring Liberation Theology or other "progressive" causes were removed from their teaching positions. Bishop Pedro Casaldágila of Brazil was called to Rome in June 1988 to explain his progressive ideas. Rules for a number of Orders for nuns were tightened and deliberalized. Complaints could be heard that the Vatican was trying to "stack" offices of religious Orders and institutions with tradition-minded individuals in preparation for the extraordinary Synod of Bishops in November, 1985.[22]

This Synod was feared by some as an apotheosis of the church's retreat from concessions made at Vatican II and from "modernism" in general. Horizontalism, collegiality, and free expression were expected to become victims of the new wave of conservatism.[23] But nothing as radical happened. Neither the fears of the progressives nor the hopes of the conservatives were confirmed. Each could find something pleasing in the conclusions of the Synod. It reflected the "spirit of conciliation" and the position of compromise so often advocated by Pope John Paul II. On Liberation Theology in particular, the Final Report reemphasized the spiritual mission of the church, including its duty to "prophetically denounce every form of poverty and oppression and everywhere defend and promote the fundamental and inalienable right of the human person."[24]

Then, the new *Instruction on Christian Freedom and Liberation* appeared in March 1986, as promised in the conversations during the Boff case. It was to be read in conjunction with the earlier *Instruction* and can therefore not be considered a rejection but a conciliatory amplification. Its greater sympathy with Liberation Theology presumably reflected the greater influence of John Paul II as well as the many bishops who, this time, were consulted during the writing of the document.

On the occasion of the publication, Cardinal Ratzinger remarked that the goal of the document was to update Roman Catholic social teaching with an eye more to ethical than political ends. In consequence, the first third of the *Instruction, 1986* dealt with the role of religion in the life of the individual, the meaning of freedom and liberation in Catholicism and, above all, the role of sin as the source of personal and social evil. It elaborated and emphasized once again the primacy of spiritual over material liberation and the need to consider material improvements in the light of the Gospel. Implied was the warning against turning Christ's teaching into a temporal, social, and economic message or guide to revolutionary action.

As the document turned more directly to material liberation, it expressly condemned Marxism and revolution (without mentioning that doctrine by name), but also condemned unbridled capitalism. It repeated the church's commitment to the poor, but not to the exclusion of other classes. Preferential option for the poor could not be expressed "by means of reductive sociology and ideological categories which would make this preference a partisan choice and a source of conflict." The new basic communities or other groups of Christians that have arisen to be witness to this evangelical love "are a great source of hope for the Church," providing they will "live in unity with the local Church and the universal Church." Catholic principles must be "the basis of *criteria for making judgments* on social situations, structures and systems." In effect, this means that human beings are responsible for the nature of their society. Improvements in the society can come only through improvements in its members, in other words, conversion. As the members build, develop, and change their society, their ethical principles: justice, the common good, social solidarity, brotherly love must be the guidelines. A "civilization of love" must be the end product. It cannot be created through hatred, class wars, violence, tyranny, or ignoring individuals. Those high principles must underlie the basic reforms of present social, political, economic systems required for the total liberation of human beings. These reforms must be brought about by the laity while the church devotes itself mainly to spiritual matters such as the foundation for improving temporal matters and the success of changes.

Inevitably in such a document ambiguities appeared. But the greater sympathy toward Liberation Theology in this document, as compared to that of 1984, was apparent. Boff and Gutiérrez welcomed it, Jon Sobrino had strong reservations. The *New York Times'* Rome correspondent, E. J. Dionne Jr. called the document a "new phase" in the pope's campaign against some forms of Liberation Theology, aiming at "blunting the political emphasis" in the Theology as presented by the more leftist theologians.[25] An adviser to Cardinal Ratzinger questioned how anyone could discern any approval of Liberation Theology in the document,[26] and Richard Neuhaus of the *National Review* agreed with him.[27] The weekly *America* complained the statement could mean all things to all people, though "it could not be otherwise, since the church's double reality—an otherworldly mystery made up of people confronting this world's problems—means it is ever poised between the twin dangers of disincarnate irrelevance and bloody ideology."[28]

While the *Instruction,* 1986 no. 61, showed less animosity to Liberation Theology, it also emphasized the church's withdrawal from politics, placing the burden of bringing about social change upon the laity because the "political and economic running of society is not a direct part of her mission."

This position permits no great hope that the church would directly and actively become instrumental in changing sinful structures. Such a lofty position might keep the church out of conflict—who could object to its high principles—but it would also clarify the dividing line from Liberation theologians sharing an equally high principled, but more activist approach to changing sinful structures.

In actuality, the church has never been able to stay out of politics, actively or passively. Self-preservation has been the base of its claim to be neutral on political regimes—as long as they were acting on unobjectionable principles. Yet, in every society questions of public policy arise on topics close to the church's interests in which the church is obliged to and does pronounce itself in the light of its general principles. That fact in itself is quite sufficient to get the church involved in politics, no matter how much the church thought that its neutrality was not compromised by such a stand. The difficulty with the church's claim to exist above politics has always been that some governments did not share its conviction that its principles or the consequences of its principles were unassailable from any standpoint. The church itself in the course of its history has interpreted and reinterpreted these principles in various ways depending upon historical circumstances. No less can be expected from governments. Therein lies the stuff of political conflict from which the church cannot stay out any more than anyone else.

The triangular relationship between the Vatican, the Liberation Theology and the U.S. government, to be discussed in the following chapter, will illustrate the inevitability or perhaps even the desirability of the church to become involved in politics. Such involvement could have constructive consequences were it triggered by concern for the poor. Documents and statements emanating from the Vatican—in some contrast to those authored by the popes—possess, however, strongly bureaucratic and ecclesiastic technical features. Their preoccupation all too often appears to be not the fate of the poor but the maintenance of Rome's preeminence in all respects. They lack the warmth and compassion permeating papal pronouncements, even when these too address themselves to Rome's central position in the Catholic church.

14

The United States and Liberation Theology

The United States' obtrusion in Latin American affairs has a long history. It affects the relationship between the United States and Liberation Theology. In general Latin Americans—unless they are "internal colonialists"—are suspicious of the motivations behind United States actions affecting their countries. North Americans are leery of any developments in Latin America potentially threatening their interests.

Most of the time, U.S. interests in Latin America were concentrated on security and economic matters. The United States was dealing with governments, the oligarchies, and the military. As long as the church cooperated more or less closely with these groups, there was no cause for a special relationship between it and the United States. U.S. interests were safe, by and large. Watchfulness by the United States was sufficient. But as that cooperation was breaking down, a changing Latin American church's interests and correspondingly those of the United States were threatening to impinge upon each other.

As soon as U.S. governments and U.S. businesses in Latin America sensed the development, U.S. interest in church affairs intensified. It was bad enough, some U.S. circles felt, that popes advocated changes in social structures. When Liberation theologians and Ecclesiastic Base Communities initiated such changes, official America became alarmed. Should they succeed, U.S. interests were no longer safe. Neither popes nor Liberation theologians had left any doubt about the contributions of all the First World to the maintenance of the sinful structures responsible for the misery of the Latin American poor. In Latin America, the United States was obviously a prime contributor.

From the beginning, official U.S. interpretation of the causes of Latin American social unrest tended to concide with that of the growing ranks of extremely conservative high church officials: not the social structures, but those who incited the poor masses against them, that is, Marxists, were basically responsible. The U.S. government could hardly have cherished the pope pointing the finger at the United States in all but name when he stated in *Sollicitudo rei socialis,* 1988 no. 21, that the East-West conflict rested on two different concepts of the development of humans and peoples, "both concepts being imperfect and in need of radical corrections," and then added that both blocs harbored a tendency toward imperialism! The pope's words had no influence on the U.S. interpretation that Marxism in Latin America was the root of all evil. This interpretation determined a priori on which side the United States would stand in the debate over Liberation Theology. U.S. governments were not troubled as were religious parties over the mixture of ingredients in theological progressivism: how much Marxism and how much authentic Catholicism was in it. To them it was beyond doubt that Marxism, no matter how much, was the danger causing anxieties in Washington and U.S. business circles. Their interest in the issue went no further.

As early as 1944, the CIA (then the OSS) had begun to watch the individual later to become Pope John XXIII because of his "leftist" tendencies.[1] After the publication of his encyclical *Pacem in terris,* 1963, surveillance was increased. Nelson Rockefeller, after his extensive tour through Latin America in 1969, warned that the Latin American church was "vulnerable to subversive penetration."[2] In 1975, CIA director William Colby was reported to have written a letter to Senator Mark Hatfield, suggesting that it was not advisable to break contacts between the CIA and national and foreign clergymen, as the clergy could be very helpful to the United States through many contacts in many countries of the world.

In 1979, testimony was given before the Senate Foreign Relations Committee that President Carter had instructed the CIA to watch activities closely in the Latin American church so that he would not be confronted with another "Iran-type" situation.[3] In 1980, the so-called Santa Fe policy statement was prepared for use by President Reagan. It identified itself with the elitist Latin American doctrine of "National Security," the codeword for the maintenance of a vertical political structure and the suppression by any means of popular participation. The document conjured up the danger of Cuban hegemony over Latin America. It demanded that the United States must "fight," not just counteract, Liberation Theology. A CIA manual uncovered n 1984, written by a "low level employee" according to administration officials, recommended coordination with the Vatican to speak of "the persecution of the Church in Nicaragua."[4]

Once elected, President Reagan wasted no time in translating the Santa Fe proposals into policies. He and his administration have shown consistent hostility to Liberation Theology and proceeded to implement it with action. For instance, in trying to win the support of the U.S. Catholic bishops, he sent a "White House Digest" to all of them in October 1984. It quoted speeches and statements of Central American bishops and other clerics, allegedly demonstrating their agreement with U.S. policy toward El Salvador. The vicar general of that country, Monsignor Ricardo Urioste, criticized the "Digest" for its wrong focus on Archbishop Rivera y Damas by citing him selectively. Other quoted statements were taken out of context.[5]

In April 1985 President Reagan announced that he had received a verbal message from Pope John Paul II urging continued U.S. efforts in Central America. The Vatican immediately denied the existence of any message either regarding the situation in Central America or U.S. activities there.[6] Secretary of State Shultz, referring to alleged support by some U.S. clergy of Marxist revolutionaries in El Salvador that, he feared, would increase Soviet influence, said "when you follow policies bound to result in that effect, that is what you are doing." Vice President Bush, supporting him, said "maybe it makes me a right-wing extremist, but I am puzzled, I just do not understand it."[7]

One of President Reagan's methods in obtaining funds from Congress and popular support for his Nicaraguan policies had been the use of language evoking strong popular antagonism against the Sandinistas (e.g. the church is being "persecuted," those who do it are "atheists," and so on). He accused the Sandinistas of supporting various rival religious factions in order to weaken the official church.

Throughout recent years, the CIA has engaged in intensive activity in Latin America (e.g. the ouster of Arbenz in Guatemala, 1954, and Allende in Chile, 1973). Of late, it has been found to subsidize books, newspapers, magazines, radio stations, political parties and candidates, and religious and research organizations considered favorable to the traditional church. It has participated in many enterprises helpful in defeating liberal secular and ecclesiastic groups. Its records on religious activities were made available to Cardinal Trujillo and Roger Vekemans. Archibishop Quinn testified before a congressional hearing committee that during a speech he was invited to give in El Salvador, three U.S. Embassy officials took notes and he felt, he said, as if he were in the Soviet Union.[8]

The Nicaraguan government has for a long time claimed that Cardinal Obando was one of the channels through which the CIA is supplying funds to the official church. But when he was interviewed about one of his propaganda and admittedly fund-raising trips to the United States, he answered "I don't know who the CIA is. Here we follow the Pope." He was interested only in helping the poor, he elaborated, not in politics.[9]

In El Salvador, the U.S. government does not support the church peace policy of keeping all foreign arms out of the country in order to achieve a broad-based political arrangement among all factions. In pursuit of that neutral policy, Archbishop Rivera y Damas announced in June, 1986, that he had refused all funds offered to him by the AID.[10] U.S. bishops have complained that the U.S. government was hampering their work on behalf of Salvadoran refugees and was not assisting U.S. church workers in obtaining visas for El Salvador because they were suspect to the Salvadoran government.

The persistent complaints of the Nicaraguan government about CIA assistance to its enemies were at least indirectly confirmed—if that was still necessary—when President Reagan in 1986 officially transferred day-to-day responsibility for managing military operations by the contras to the CIA and Vice President Bush confirmed CIA aid to the contras. Fernando Cardenal, Nicaragua's minister for education, frequently remarked on the anti-Sandinista activities of the CIA and on the parallelism between U.S. and Vatican policies. "From our vantage point, the political stance of the Vatican toward Nicaragua coincides with that of President Reagan."[11]

Within the United States the work of the CIA was complemented by FBI activities. The institution admitted keeping records on the "peace" bishops Hunthausen (Seattle) and Gumbleto (Detroit).[12] FBI spies had infiltrated church groups opposed to the U.S. policy in Latin America. An FBI agent resigned from the agency because he was asked to investigate nonviolent peace activists.[13]

Additional funds to those supplied by AID and the CIA came from many U.S. quarters. Well-endowed religious foundations and U.S. corporations have poured money into Latin America to weaken liberal trends. An internal memorandum of a major U.S. corporation with extensive interests in Latin America disclosed many activities of itself and other corporations in favor of conservative religious groups and churches.

Archbishop Hickey[14] testified before a congressional subcommittee in 1983, "A most recent and very disturbing development . . . is the emergence of sectarian churches called Protestant but decidedly not representing the mainline Protestant churches. These sects are militantly anti-Catholic, very conservative politically and are welcomed and cultivated by right-wing elements"—in and out of government—in El Salvador and Honduras as a counterweight to the Catholic's social witness. In the same year, the Latin American Bishops Conference reported the same phenomenon as part of a larger political design, conceived by U.S. conservatives who wanted to stem the social progress supported by the Catholic church, and it decided to fight this development. Nevertheless, Mexico's bishops reported 45 million had been "lured" away from the Catholic church. Fundamentalists claimed 10-15 percent of the Latin American population.[15]

Other, always private, groups in the United States are strongly supporting Liberation Theology and Base Communities. Their work appears to be more public and less well financed. Several religious orders have openly and repeatedly confirmed their support for Liberation Theology, the communities, and the People's church. Senator Denton held hearings of a U.S. Senate subcommittee on "marxism and Christianity in Revolutionary Central America" in October 1983. He opened the hearings with the statement that Liberation Theology was a form of "syncretic merger of Marxism and Christianity which could strongly assist marxist and Sandinista guerrillas, using well-meaning and sincere religious groups who wanted to better the lot of the poor." Latin American refugee religious testified that the Theology had become "an integral part of the subversive movement through which Cuba and the Soviet Union intend to destabilize and ultimately conquer the 'soft underbelly' of the United States." They claimed that ample funds were supporting the movement, coming "from a well financed network of centers and publishing houses," of which five were in Washington, D.C., alone.[16]

A very important event affecting the relations between the United States and the church in Rome as well as Latin America occurred in January 1984. The president's "personal representative" became ambassador to the Vatican. Diplomatic relations were restored. The step had been preceded by President Reagan's visit to the pope in January 1983. A communiqué at that time stated "one of the areas of our mutual concern is Latin America. We want to work closely with the church in that area to help promote peace, social justice and reform to prevent the spread of repression and godless tyranny."[17]

The main senatorial sponsor of the appointment of an ambassador was Senator Richard Lugar. He felt it would be "good for U.S. diplomacy and security." During Senate hearings on the measure and on the appointment of William Wilson as ambassador (since replaced), the senator, the ambassador and various State Department officials referred to the Vatican's involvement in international affairs; the pope as a powerful force for the political and moral values "which we in the United States cherish"; the "Holy See's" access to areas of great concern to U.S. foreign policy, including Latin America; the Vatican's usefulness as a listening post for international events and developments; and the Vatican's influence in many countries not just on religious but on a wide range of social issues. The ambassador's role was to discuss "questions of war and peace," not religion.[18]

What the ambassador's role was at the Vatican in regard to Liberation Theology became clear after an interview he gave to the National Catholic News Service in November 1984. He confirmed that the United States was trying to stay away from theology, philosophy, and religion, and to stick to political and military facts. He also confirmed that the Reagan administration had become concerned over Liberation Theology and so had the embassy. This concern "stems from the administration's concerns with respect to having another Marxist nation. We're trying to contain the spread of Marxism" in connection with which the political and military tensions in Latin America were a cause of concern. He praised the *Instruction*, 1984, because "We thought the time had arrived when the world was interested in hearing what the Vatican had to say on Liberation theology."[19]

U.S. sympathy with forces opposed to Liberation Theology is true to the pattern of U.S. policy in Latin America. Concern for security and the welfare of U.S. corporations has usually determined who the recipients of U.S. support would be. They usually belonged to the most reactionary groups available. Public U.S. money flowing to governments and groups antagonistic to Liberation Theology has little to do with religion and much with its feared political implications. The thrust of U.S. governments' dealing with religious progressivism in Latin America since the end of World War II, and especially since Medellín, has been generally to strengthen conservatism and reaction wherever they could be found. In effect, this amounts to a policy detrimental to the poor. As elsewhere in the world, so in Latin America, the outstanding quality of recent United States governments has been to misread the signs of the times.

This U.S. policy could have the effect of a self-fulfilling prophecy in the very long run. It has been unable to stop the expansion of Liberation Theology and the spread of Ecclesiastical Base Communities, probably only helped to slow their pace. Neither the Theology nor the communities are revolutionary. They are not envisaging change through revolution. But when the rich continue to get richer and the poor poorer, when "international financial imperialism" chokes social and economic development, enough explosive material may accumulate to bring about social changes far beyond the plans of progressive churchmen and politicians. Washington's Latin American policies forces them into the least desired option.

A redeeming feature in U.S.–Latin American relations are the efforts of nongovernmental agencies to assist the modernization and development of the Latin American poor. Thousands of U.S. citizens have gone especially to Central America to demonstrate their goodwill toward the Latin American peoples and manifest their disagreements with U.S. policy. In the United States many churches have converted themselves into sanctuaries for the reception of refugees fleeing from persecution in their home countries. U.S. bishops have sharply criticized U.S. policy. U.S. religious organizations have mobilized large crowds for demonstrations to protest U.S. policy in Central America. These activities are not likely to balance the massive assistance coming from the U.S. government, the public international agencies it greatly influences, and U.S. business. They show, at least, that the U.S. ideals of human dignity and human rights have defenders in the United States.

Epilogue

The central position poverty has assumed in the contemporary Catholic church is surprising mainly because of the inferior position it was given in the recent past. The relative neglect of this issue in the "church of the poor" had many causes. The church was too much involved in secular politics. Fighting to acquire or maintain mundane power attracted too much attention and consumed too many resources. Bureaucratization of the church conduced to administrative efficiency at the expense of humane concerns. Routine replaced religious responsibility. Association with ruling classes relegated awareness of existing poverty into the subconscious. Alms giving would further relieve pangs of conscience. When poverty was defined as lack of material goods and an individual's problem, the church's primary mission of salvation could lead to complacency. The recognition became lost that poverty, properly and broadly understood in the Gospel sense, was a most suitable condition for exercising and developing Christian virtues, benefiting the poor as well as all Christians identifying themselves with the poor.

The poverty coming with the industrial revolution, the emergence of the Third World with its poor masses, the growth of human rights into prominence conspired to bring the problem of poverty to the fore. People began asking again what it meant to be human, to be part of the brotherhood of man, to be one's brother's keeper. One answer was, in one form or another, that it meant to identify with the neighbor, to be coresponsible for him or her, especially the poor and the suffering. Such a solidarity with the poor, said Sobrino and other Liberation theologians, was an ethical demand upon the individual as well as salvific.

In this sense, aiding the poor goes beyond material improvement of the person. It enters the realm of the spiritual: for the recipient by helping his liberation, for the donor by giving meaning to life. In choosing the preferential option for the poor, the church has reaffirmed its commitment to the poor. It has made itself the symbol of the poor. It has also de-Europeanized itself and is living up to the universality of its nature. The Liberation theologians insist that in this manner the church shows what it means to be church today. And it also shows what it means to be human today. Turning to the poor, suffering, sharing, and identifying with them is the road leading to the brotherhood of man and the unity of the church.

To First World theologians and the Vatican in Rome, this strong emphasis upon poverty as almost the sole, certainly the main foundation of the Catholic religion, the church and theology may seem unduly restrictive. The fact is, however, that also in rich countries the problem of poverty is playing a major role. In the "Pastoral Letter on Catholic Teaching and the U.S. Economy," approved by the National Conference of Catholic Bishops on November 13, 1986,[1] the U.S. episcopate once again stressed the need to improve economic conditions for the poor within and without the country. "The church has a special call to be the servant of the poor, the sick and the marginalized, thereby becoming a true sign of the church's mission—a mission shared by every member of the Christian community." "Part of the American dream has been to make this world a better place to live in; at this moment of history this dream must include everyone on this globe. Since we profess to be members of a 'catholic' or universal Church we all must raise our sights to a concern for the well-being of everyone in the world." The economic interdependence across the earth must be seen "as a moment of grace—a 'kairos'—that can unite all of us in a common community of the human family. We commit ourselves to this global vision." Similarly, in Germany in 1984 a group "Initiative Kirche von unten," comprising several progressive groups of Catholics, organized a "Night of Solidarity" at which Cardinal Lorscheider of Brazil spoke, and publishes appeals for cooperation with the Third World. Such activities can be found in Switzerland, Australia, and many other countries of the First World.

In the light of basic agreement on such fundamental aspects of the church, disagreement on means or their theologic foundation should not destroy the existing unity. Actually, during the last two centuries, church, theologians, and some clergy and religious were not as far apart as they sometimes thought they were. In spite of controversy and occasional punitive church action, they all influenced each other, sooner or later. Assuming goodwill on the part of all concerned, Liberation Theology is a danger to the unity of the church only if the church makes it so.

At the present time, three elements propel the tendency toward unity. The first, and perhaps the most important, is agreement on the preferential option for the poor. The second is the scarcity of time. The official church cannot wait, as it did in the nineteenth century, for a hundred years before adjusting to new social conditions. The third is that seemingly differing theologies have, in fact, many similarities, including aspects of socialism. Differences within the Catholic church can be and have been tolerated. As long as fundamental religious principles are not violated, such diversity should be unobjectionable, if not necessary. The Magisterium teaches that in different parts of the world or in different cultures, the same goal may be reached along different paths, similar problems may have to be solved in different ways.

This lesson has particular importance for Latin America and other parts of the Third World. Liberation theology has developed out of an historical experience. The theologians have reflected on the Good News of the Evangelium from the perspective of and in solidarity with the poor. Their conclusions do not divert from the reflections of others to a very large degree. On the most important question of poverty, as this study shows, there has been a rapprochement between the various positions taken by the official church, theologians, clergy, and religious dealing with this problem.

All parties claim the Gospel as the foundation for their conclusions. If there is a readiness for agreement, this should provide some ground for it. There is agreement on the fundamentals of Catholic teaching. Controversies which existed did not lead to schisms. Bishop Casaldágila, referring to the excommunicated Bishop Lefebvre of Switzerland, said, "Schism will not come from Latin America, but from Ecône."[2] On the contrary, in the course of time mutual adjustments were achieved. What, for instance, appeared as a daring advance by early nineteenth century theologians has long been overtaken by the Magisterium of the twentieth century. There is far-reaching agreement also on the concept of liberation, summed up in the term *integral liberation,* and what its religious function is as a stage toward salvation.

There still remains much controversy about the influence of socialism on Liberation Theology. The church would have reason to worry if the theologians suggested some orthodox Marxism, based on atheistic ideology, envisaging the establishment of a totalitarian society as the end of human striving for perfection, and if this society were to be reached by violent means. No theologian is going to any such extreme, and only one or two approach it. Yet this is the extremist form of socialism the

Vatican is imputing to all Liberation theologians, ignoring thereby the many features the social encyclicals share with some forms of socialism. If the church would go further than it does in projecting the model of a future society for which recent encyclicals were to be used as blueprints, that society would reflect much influence of socialism on its builders.

There remains the church's worry about the theologians' use of what it calls the use of Marxist methodology in analyzing society. This methodology might be dangerous to the church only if it is accepted in its reductionist form and totality, for instance by accepting historic materialism as the explanation of human reality, defining human personality as a result of earthly environment, denying any transcendental effect upon human beings and human affairs. Liberation theologians are not doing this. There are features of Marxist social analysis able to stand by themselves. Certain aspects of capitalist society—poverty and inequality, the class struggle, the profit motive—can be explanatory without having to lead to an acceptance of Marxist solutions of social problems, or a Marxist society, or a Marxist interpretation of human nature. "Marxist methodology" need basically be no more than a systematic examination of the facts making up in their totality the nature and functioning of a given society (though what weight is given to these factors is another matter!). When some popes came to the conclusion that in addition to sinful men also sinful structures were responsible (i.e. collective sin) for poverty, they reached this conclusion not as a result of divine inspiration or some preconceived ideology, but by examining closely the nature of capitalist society. The desirable effect of the controversy over methodology has been for all parties to realize the importance of the social sciences also for a proper application of the gospel to contemporary social conditions.

There are other issues causing disputes between the church and Liberation theologians. For instance the role of the state in dealing with poverty, the balance, between spirituality and materialism in the process of evangelization, the extent to which politicization should be a churchly function. As this study demonstrates, these matters represent in practice no serious hindrance to an understanding between the official church and Liberation theologians from any doctrinal standpoint. They are frequently ecclesiastic-political issues. The church may perceive an intolerable challenge to its central power when Liberation theologians sometimes assume functions or encourage others to assume functions which it believes are legitimately within its jurisdiction. They are sometimes also issues which the Liberation theologians conceive as local or regional, but where the church apprehends global consequences. The Liberation theologians are not alone when, in the name of collegiality, they request participation in decision making. "Horizontalism" is a demand to be found in all geographic sections of the church.

These issues, in other words, are often of a temporary nature, not relating to basic incompatible positions, or eventually becoming compatible positions. The flexibility of the parties is safeguarded if both follow Pope John XXIII's prescription in his opening address of Vatican II: "What is needed is that this certain and immutable doctrine to which the faithful owe obedience, be studied afresh and reformulated in contemporary terms. For this deposit of faith, or truths which are contained in our time-honored teaching is one thing; the manner in which these truths are set forth (with their meaning preserved intact) is something else."[3]

Unfortunately for the fate of the poor in Latin America (and elsewhere) secular and ecclesiastic politics are taking up a considerable amount of time and effort of church and theologians. Both are prevented from devoting all their energies to the poor. The theoretical position of the church has undergone enormous change since the beginning of the nineteenth century. Yet, all too often secular and self-created ecclesiastic political problems have impeded it from doing much more than it has always done for the poor—and that was too little.

The church could act more than merely appealing in accordance with its knowledge about the causes of poverty, especially in an area like Latin America where its influence on politics is great. The church's reticence has contributed to the fact, established by the encyclicals, that the rich are getting richer and the poor poorer. Its attitude had lost it a large section of its following, by default, in the nineteenth century to other social movements. There is little excuse now to repeat that same mistake in the Third World. Reliance on Catholic political parties is insufficient. They may or sometimes may not act under the influence of the church. To what extent they do, is doubtful. Changing social structures, at any rate, is not in their program. The least it could do would be to give free rein to those seeing in the Gospel a command to act and to follow it.

The barriers some sections of the hierarchy in Rome and Latin America place in the way of the Liberation theologians, is ominously reminiscent of the method the church used in the nineteenth century. Hindering or even punishing the theologians seeking Christian answers to the problem of poverty instead of those "sinfully" causing the problem seems punishing the wrong people. It is also antagonizing the increasing following of Liberation Theology. The church is attracting new members to the priesthood in Latin America, partly as a result of Liberation Theology and its promise of concrete changes, it is widely held. Pope John Paul II has praised the Base Communities, encouraged the progressive bishops of Brazil to continue their good work. High clergy in many parts of the world are eager to accommodate the Magisterium to modern conditions. Clearly, the progressivism in the church of which the Liberation theologians represent an important part, is making the church relevant to more and more people. Yet, in Latin America and elsewhere, the Vatican, with the help of conservative clergy, is denigrating and counteracting the theologians. It is everywhere limiting the freedom of action of progressive clergy.

Liberation theologians do not have all the answers. At least they are action oriented. Their activities and those of the Base Communities have already produced leaders and numerous social organizations. More can be expected. The members of the communities are described as high in spirit and confident of the future. This is in itself a valuable change and an opportunity for the church. The very existence of the communities is a fulfillment of the demand for "association," "community," and "solidarity," voiced so many times and for so long by popes and clergy.

Liberation Theology is not yet a finished doctrine. It is underdeveloped in many ways (e.g. the role of women, methods for social change, and so on). It may never become a comprehensive doctrine, due to its close relationship both to local conditions and the changing signs of the times. The theologians hardly conceive of it as a comprehensive doctrine, certainly not an independent one. To them, it is their interpretation of the Gospel on the basis of Catholic principles. Their major contribution is to have placed the earthly, material aspects of the Theology into the context of the Gospel. No theologian hereafter is likely to find a way of limiting the Gospel to purely spiritual matters or of returning to mere alms giving as the fulfillment of Christian duties toward the neighbor. Nor will theology serve as an excuse for inactivity in this world.

For these reasons, not merely because it is widely popular, is it likely to survive. Popes, cardinals, bishops, priests, and nuns accept the Theology's fundamental principles. Division exists mostly over the means by which to bring about liberation. Resistance comes mostly from those who need earthly liberation the least, which is, indeed, the reason why the Theology has also become a secular political issue.

It is unfortunate but was inevitable that the passions of nationalism and civil wars have become immixed in the debate over the Theology. They have affected the positions of the parties to the debate and aggravated the Theology's political implications. At the same time, however, the causes producing nationalism and civil wars have also been among the causes producing and popularizing the Theology. They should not be ignored because they demonstrate, once again, how relevant the meaning of the Gospel can be to historical conditions.

Basically, however, Liberation Theology can exist and survive on its own grounds. Moreover, its roots in nineteenth century progressive theology will further safeguard its survival. It is not a fad nor a theological chimera. Most likely, as time passes, it will share the fate of that older theology by becoming a part of the Magisterium. This is a matter of time and, for the sake of the poor, it may be hoped not too long a time. Adoption or cooption of the Theology by the official church is not an impossibility. There are precedents. Incorporation of the Theology into official church doctrine would settle the controversy. It would avoid the danger of splits, expand the church's ecumenicity, maintain the hierarchical structure in the more liberal spirit of Vatican II, bring about the much desired reconciliation, and benefit the poor.

Notes

The following abbreviations are used in the notes: KIPA = Katholische Internationale Presse Agentur (Fribourg, Switzerland); *NYT* = *New York Times;* *NCR* = *National Catholic Reporter.* In the footnotes, only authors and pages are cited. The complete titles of their books will be found in the Bibliography.

CHAPTER 1

1. Kaiser, p. 89.
2. Whyte, p. 108.
3. *NCR,* November 14, 1986.

CHAPTER 2

1. Collins, p. 15.
2. The account of the situation in France relies heavily on Collins, Duroselle, Maier, Moody, ed.
3. The account of the situation in Germany relies heavily on Moody, ed., Sperber, Spotts.
4. Reprinted in Moody, ed., pp. 536-539.

CHAPTER 3

1. Coste, p. 69.
2. Rahner, vol. III, pp. 268-274; vol. VIII, pp. 168-214; Gutiérrez, p. 300.
3. Haight, p. 16.

CHAPTER 5

1. Planas, p. 61.
2. The Medellín documents can be found in CELAM, *La Iglesia en la Actual Transformación de America Latina a la Luz del Concilio, vol. II – Conclusiones,* cited by Berryman, 1987, p. 210.
3. The Puebla Conference documents can be found in Eagleson and Scharper, eds.
4. Eagleson and Scharper, eds., p. 128.
5. Blanchard, p. 22.
6. Gutiérrez, p. 26.
7. Quoted in Ferm (1986), p. 49.

CHAPTER 7

1. Smith, p. 25, 68.
2. Whyte, pp. 107-108.
3. Whyte, pp. 26-99.
4. Whyte, p. 31.
5. Riga, pp. 34, 43, 139.

CHAPTER 8

1. Collins, p. 93.
2. Alexander, pp. 540-541.
3. Moody, p. 130; Alexander, p. 408.

CHAPTER 9

1. Gutiérrez, p. 238.
2. West, p. 331.
3. Quoted in Ferm (1986), p. 49.
4. Eagleson and Scharper, eds., p. 128.
5. Gutiérrez, p. 275. See also Novak (1986), pp. 405-432.
6. Castañeda, p. 743; *NYT,* September 4, 1983.
7. *NYT,* September 4, 1983; Blanchard, pp. 25, 28, 30.
8. O'Donohue, p. 226.
9. Boff, p. 4.
10. Eagleson and Scharper, eds., p. 135.
11. Gutiérrez, p. 49.
12. *NCR,* May 31, 1985.
13. Levine, ed., passim, especially pp. 3-8, 187-192, 236-238; Klaiber, pp. 2-3; Maloney, p. 52; Berryman, pp. 10-11; Brockma, pp. 931-935; Lernoux, p. 383; Mainwaring, 1986b, passim.
14. Castañeda, p. 739.
15. *NYT,* May 8, 15, 1988.

CHAPTER 10

1. Dirks, p. 682.
2. Braaten, p. 144.
3. Compare Ferm (1986), pp. 115-117.

PART II

1. Daniel-Rops (1965b), p. 185.
2. Câmara, *NCR*, January 22, 1988; Gutiérrez, *Folhetim* (São Paulo), December 29, 1985.
3. See footnote 13, Chapter 9.
4. *Le Monde*, August 9, 1985.
5. MacEoin (1987); *NCR*, May 5, 1987.
6. Kramer, pp. 40-75.

CHAPTER 11

1. *NCR*, May 3, 1983.
2. *NCR*, December 28, 1984.
3. Compare Montgomery, pp. 209-210, 219-220; Libby, p. 82.
4. *NCR*, November 18, 1983.
5. Libby, p. 85; *NCR*, April 2, 1982, June 20, 1986.
6. *NCR*, December 28, 1984.
7. Shiras, pp. 227-228.
8. *NCR*, May 22, 1987.
9. *NCR*, November 27, 1987; April 22, 1988.
10. U.S. Department of State, Bureau of Public Affairs, Special Report #10, March 1987, p. 7.
11. MacEoin (1984), pp. 294-299.
12. *Current Digest of the Soviet Press*, vol. 30 #40, June, 1984, pp. 12-13.
13. Williams, pp. 341-369; MacEoin (1984), p. 295.
14. Greinacher, ed., pp. 280-299.
15. *NYT*, August 1, 1984; *NCR*, March 7, 1986.
16. *NCR*, August 14, 1987.
17. MacEoin (1987); *NCR*, May 5, 1987; Williams, p. 365.
18. *NCR*, February 14, 1986.
19. Dodson, pp. 79-105.
20. O'Brien, pp. 50-72.
21. *Tages Anzeiger* (Zürich), December 19, 1984.
22. *NCR*, May 28, 1982; December 21, 1984; January 11, 1985; Martin, pp. 65, 113, 134.
23. *NCR*, January 11, 1985.
24. *Tages Anzeiger* (Zürich), February 6, 1985.
25. *Le Monde*, July 9, 1985; August 6, 1985.
26. *Die Zeit*, August 6, 1985; see also Casaldágila's interview with *El Pais* (Madrid), June 20, 1988.

27. *Osservatore Romano* (English edition), February 24, 1986; *NCR,* February 7, 1986.

28. *NCR,* February 7; August 15, 1986.

29. *NCR,* August 15, 1986; August 15, 1987.

30. *Weltwoche* (Zürich), July 11, 1985.

31. *NCR,* May 23, 1986.

32. MacEoin (1987); *NCR,* April 25, 1986; Reding, p. 36; Cardinal Danneels, Columbia Network TV interview, January 25, 1986.

33. *NCR,* April 11, 1986; January 30, May 22, 1987.

34. *NCR,* February 14, 1986.

35. *NCR,* May 16, 1986; August 26, 1988.

36. Compare Reding, pp. 25-30.

37. *NCR,* November 20, 1981.

38. *NCR,* November 20, 1981.

39. Bowen, pp. 726-727.

40. Compare Ferm (1986), pp. 13, 17; Berryman, pp. 17-18, 21; *NCR,* October 23, 1987.

41. Levine, pp. 187-217.

42. Compare Klaiber, passim.

43. *NCR,* October 12, 1984.

44. *NCR,* October 5, 1984.

45. *NCR,* February 1, 1985.

46. *Paginas,* 1984.

47. *NYT,* February 12, 1985.

48. *NCR,* February 15, 1985; April 12, 1985. See also Scheetz, *NCR* October 12, 1984.

49. *NCR,* April 11, 1986; May 15, 1987.

50. KIPA, April 24, 1984; *Publik-Forum* (Frankfurt/Main), August 24, 1984, p. 4.

51. KIPA, October 14, 1983.

52. *Weltwoche* (Zürich), June 26, 1986; *NCR,* June 19, 1987.

53. *NCR,* March 14, 1986; March 21, 1986.

54. *NCR,* April 22, 1986.

55. Bruneau (1986), pp. 106-123; *Le Monde,* June 28, 1985.

56. *Publik-Forum* (Frankfurt/Main), June 20, 1986, p. 2.

57. *Frankfurter Allgemeine Zeitung,* July 8, 1986; *NCR,* November 27, 1987.

58. *Guardian* (London), April 20, 1986.

59. Compare Smith (1982), passim.

60. Arellano, pp. 397-418.

61. Turner, pp. 27-31.

62. Cited in Gutiérrez, p. 113.

63. Loveman, pp. 6-8.

64. Smith (1986), pp. 156-186.

65. *America,* June 14, 1986, p. 484.

66. Loveman, pp. 6-8.

67. *NCR,* January 15, 1988; *Frankfurter Allgemeine Zeitung,* June 14, 1988.

68. Compare Ruiz, p. 15.

CHAPTER 12

1. *Facts on File,* 1974, p. 989.

2. Eagleson and Scharper, eds., p. 60.

3. Peerman (1979b), p. 204.

4. Eagleson and Scharper, eds., pp. 81-83.

5. *Le Nouvel Observateur* (Paris), August 2, 1985, p. 64. See Donders, *Afrikanische Befreiungstheologie,* passim.

6. *NCR,* September 30, 1983.

7. *NCR,* March 25, 1983; Zeller, pp. 2-3.

8. *NYT,* February 6, 1985; see also February 2, 3, 5, 7, 8, 10, 1985, for details of the pope's speeches.

9. *NCR,* February 8, 1985.

10. See *NCR,* February 8, 15, 1985; *Facts on File,* 1985, p. 61, for details of the pope's speeches.

11. *NCR,* October 26, 1985.

12. *NYT,* November 19, 1984.

13. *NYT,* October 26, 1984.

14. *NCR,* February 1, 1985.

15. *NCR,* April 12, 1985.

CHAPTER 13

1. *Frankfurter Allgemeine Zeitung,* July 7, 1987.

2. Greinacher, ed., pp. 98-105.

3. Peerman, (1979b), p. 374; see also *Frankfurter Allgemeine Zeitung,* July 8, 1986.

4. *NCR,* May 14, 1982.

5. *Der Spiegel,* #20, 1985, p. 146.

6. *Der Spiegel,* #38, 1984, p. 157.

7. *Osservatore Romano* (English edition), September 10, 1984.

8. *Osservatore Romano* (English edition), September 10, 1984.

9. *Die Zeit,* September 7, 1984.

10. *NYT,* November 24, 1984.

11. *NYT,* September 18, 1984.

12. *NYT,* February 12, 1985.

13. *NCR,* September 14, 1984.

14. Many reactions were reported in the *NYT, NCR* and KIPA of that period.

15. Text in *El Mercurio* (Medellín), January 29, 1985; *Frankfurter Allgemeine Zeitung,* August 2, 1985.

16. Boff, Leonardo and Clodovis, pp. 223-233; *NCR,* December 12, 1984. The Boff case is discussed in detail also in *NCR, NYT, Osservatore Romano* (English edition) of the period.

17. October 11, 1985.

18. *NCR,* January 16, 1987.

19. These remarks were typical. Compare *NCR,* September 21, 1984; January 11, August 30, 1985.

20. *Publik-Forum* (Frankfurt/Main), August 24, 1984, p. 4; KIPA, August 16, 1984.

21. *Tages Anzeiger* (Zürich), September 8, 9, 1984.

22. *Die Zeit,* October 11, 1985; *NCR,* May 31, 1985; *El Pais,* Madrid, June 17, 19, 20, 23, 1988.

23. Compare, for example, *Le Monde,* June 27, 1985; August 8, 1985; *NYT Magazine,* November 24, 1985; *NYT,* November 30, 1985.

24. *The Extraordinary Synod—1985,* p. 65.

25. *Herald Tribune,* April 5, 6, 1986.

26. *NYT,* April 6, 1986. Cardinal Ratzinger accused Bishop Casaldágila of having called the 1986 *Instruction* a "correction" of the 1984 *Instruction. El Pais* (Madrid), June 22, 1988.

27. *National Review,* May 23, 1986, p. 37.

28. April 19, 1986, p. 314.

CHAPTER 14

1. *NCR,* December 30, 1987.

2. MacEoin (1984), p. 296.

3. *Weltwoche* (Zürich), August 23, 1984.

4. *Tages Anzeiger* (Zürich), December 19, 1984.

5. *NCR,* February 1, 1985.

6. *Honolulu Advertiser,* April 19, 1985; *Facts on File,* April 18, 1985.

7. "U.S. Policy in El Salvador," Hearings before the Subcommittee on Human Rights and International Organizations and on Western Hemisphere Affairs of the Committee on Foreign Affairs. House of Representatives. Ninety-eighth Congress, 1st Session. Third Presidential Certification on El Salvador. February 4, 28, March 7, 17, 1983, p. 231.

8. "The Air War and Political Developments in El Salvador." Hearings before the Subcommittee on Western Hemisphere Affairs of the Committee on Foreign Affairs, House of Representatives. Ninety-ninth Congress, 2nd Session, May 14, 1986, p. 86.

9. *NCR,* August 31, 1984. For details of United States' and other foreign interest groups' activities in Latin America, see Lernoux, pp. 203-310.

10. *NCR,* June 20, 1986; *Christian Century,* March 23, 30, 1983, p. 266.

11. *NCR,* January 11, 1985.

12. *NCR,* October 10, 1987.

13. *NCR,* February 5, 1988; *NYT,* November 6, 1983; *America,* December 17, 1983; *Civil Liberties,* Winter 1988, #363.

14. "U.S. Policy in El Salvador." Hearings before the Senate Subcommittee on Human Rights and International Organizations and on Western Hemisphere Affairs of the Committee on Foreign Affairs. House of Representatives. Ninety-eighth Congress, 1st Session. Third Presidential Certification on El Salvador. February 4, 28, March 7, 17, 1983, p. 202.

15. *Economist,* April 12, 1986, p. 43; *NYT,* March 16, 1983.

16. Hearings before the Subcommittee on Security and Terrorism of the Committee on the Judiciary, U.S. Senate. Ninety-eighth Congress 1st Session. "Marxism and Christianity in Revolutionary Central America," October 18-19, 1983, pp. 2, 6, 7, 8, 13-18, 108-115.

17. *NYT,* June 8, 1982; January 20, 1984; August 2, 1984.

18. Departments of Commerce, Justice, State, the Judiciary and Related Agencies. Appropriations for 1984. Hearings before a Subcommittee of the Committee on Appropriations. House of Representatives. Ninety-eighth Congress, 2nd Session, part 10, 1984, pp. 12, 28, 32, 33-34; Hearings before the Committee of Foreign Relations, U.S. Senate. Ninety-eighth Congress, 2nd Session, 1984, p. 3.

19. *NCR,* December 7, 1984.

EPILOGUE

1. National Conference of Catholic Bishops, Washington, D.C.

2. *El Pais,* Madrid, June 20, 1988.

3. Kaiser, p. 89.

Bibliography

Among the materials that have been very useful in preparing this book are those listed in the Bibliography. Articles appearing in daily and weekly newspapers are listed in the Notes, but not in the Bibliography. Also not listed in the Bibliography are the papal encyclicals and the writings of Liberation theologians— unless one is cited at length—especially Hugo Assmann, Leonardo Boff, Enrique Dussell, José M. Bonino, Gustavo Gutiérrez, José Miranda, Juan L. Segundo, Jon Sobrino. Quotations from the papal encyclicals and letters, apostolic exhortations and so on, are taken from Claudia Carlen, *The Papal Encyclicals* (Wilmington, NC: McGrath Publishing Co., 1981, 5 volumes); the St. Paul Editions (Boston); and the Libreria Editrice Vaticana (Vatican City).

Abbot, Walter M., ed. *The Vatican Council II 1962-1965*. New York: Guild, 1966.

Adriance, Madeleine. *Opting for the Poor: Brazilian Catholicism in Transition*. Kansas City, MO: Sheed & Ward, 1986.

Alexander, Edgar. "Church and Society in Germany" (325-583), in Joseph N. Moody, ed. *Church and Society: Catholic Social and Political Thought and Movements, 1789-1950*. New York: Arts, 1953.

Arellano, José-Pablo. "Social Politics in Chile: An Historical Review," *Journal of Latin American Studies*. November 1985, 397-418.

Baum, Gregory. *Religion and Alienation*. New York: Paulist, 1975.

Bentley, James. *Between Marx and Christ*. London: Verso & NLB, 1982.

Berryman, Phillip. *Liberation Theology*. New York: Pantheon, 1987.

Berryman, Phillip. "El Salvador: From Evangelization to Insurrection" (58-78), in Daniel H. Levine. *Religion and Political Conflict in Latin America*. Chapel Hill: University of North Carolina Press, 1986.

Blanchard, Paul. *Paul Blanchard on Vatican II*. Boston: Beacon, 1966.

Boff, Clodovis, and Pixley, Jorge. *Die Option für die Armen* (Düsseldorf: Patmos, 1987).

Boff, Leonardo. *Ecclesiogenesis*. Maryknoll, NY: Orbis, 1986.

Boff, Leonardo, and Boff, Clodovis. "Summons to Rome," in Hans Küng and Leonard Swidler, eds. *The Church in Anguish*. San Francisco: Harper & Row, 1986.

Bowen, Gordon L. "Four Candles in the Wind," *Commonweal*, December 18, 1987, 726-727.

Braaten, Carl E. *The Future of God*. New York: Harper & Row, 1969.

Brockma, James R. "The Prophetic Role of the Church in Latin America," *Christian Century*, October 19, 1983, 931-935.

Brown, Robert M. "Drinking from Our Wells," *Christian Century*, May 9, 1984, 483-486.

Brown, Robert M. *Theology in a New Key: Responding to Liberation Themes*. Philadelphia: Westminster, 1978.

Bruneau, Thomas C. "Brazil: The Catholic Church and Basic Christian Communities" (106-123), in Daniel H. Levine, *Religion and Political Conflict in Latin America*. Chapel Hill: University of North Carolina Press, 1986.

Bruneau, Thomas C. *The Church in Brazil: The Politics of Religion*. Austin: University of Texas Press, 1982.

Castañeda, Carlos E. "Social Developments and Movements in Latin America" (733-773), in Joseph N. Moody, ed., *Church and Society: Catholic Social and Political Thought and Movements, 1789-1950*. New York: Arts, 1953.

CELAM. *Liberacíon: Diálogos en el CELAM*. Bogotá, Colombia: CELAM, 1974.

Cleary, Edward L. *Crisis and Change. The Church in Latin America Today*. Maryknoll, NY: Orbis, 1985.

Collins, Ross W. *Catholicism and the Second French Republic*. New York: Octagon, 1980.

Coste, René. *Marxist Analysis and Christian Faith*. Maryknoll, NY: Orbis, 1985.

Currier, Fred J. "Liberation Theology and Marxist Economics," *Monthly Review*, January 1987, 24-39.

Daniel-Rops, Henri. *The Church in an Age of Revolution*. New York: E. P. Dutton, 1965a.

Daniel-Rops, Henri. *A Fight for God*. New York: E. P. Dutton, 1965b.

Dirks, Walter. "King oder Che? Am Beginn eines christlichen Dilemmas," *Frankfurter Hefte* 1968, 681-688.

Dodson, Michael. "Nicaragua: The Struggle for the Church" (79-105), in Daniel H. Levine, ed., *Religion and Political Conflict in Latin America*. Chapel Hill: University of North Carolina Press, 1986.

Donders, Joseph G. *Afrikanische Befreiungstheologie*. Olten, Switzerland: Walter, 1988.

Duroselle, Jean-Baptiste. *Les débuts du Catholicism social en France*. Paris: Presses Universitaires de France, 1951.

Eagleson, John, ed. *Christians and Socialism*. Maryknoll, NY: Orbis, 1975.

Eagleson, John, and Scharper, Philip, eds. *Puebla and Beyond*. Maryknoll, NY: Orbis, 1979.

Eicher, Peter, ed. *Theologie der Befreiung im Gespräch*. München: Kösel, 1985.

Extraordinary Synod–1985. Boston: St. Paul Editions, n.d.

Ferm, Deane W. *Third World Liberation Theologies*. Maryknoll, NY: Orbis, 1986.

Ferm, Deane W. "Outlining Rice-Roots Theology," *Christian Century*, January 25, 1984, 78-80.

Goldstein, Horst, ed. *Befreiungstheologie als Herausforderung*. Düsseldorf: Patmos, 1981.

Greinacher, Norbert, ed. *Konflikt um die Theologie der Befreiung*. Zürich: Benziger, 1985.

Gutiérrez, Gustavo. *A Theology of Liberation: History, Politics and Salvation*. Maryknoll, NY: Orbis, 1973.

Haight, Roger. *An Alternative Vision: An Interpretation of Liberation Theology*. New York: Paulist Press, 1985.

Hales, Edward E. Y. *Revolution and Papacy 1769-1846*. London: Eyre & Spottswood, 1960.

Hanks, Thomas D. *God So Loved the Third World*. Maryknoll, NY: Orbis, 1983.

Hasenhüttl, Gotthold. *Freiheit in Fesseln*. Olten, Switzerland: Walter, 1985.

Hastings, Adrian. *A Concise Guide to the Documents of the Second Vatican Council*. London: Darton, Longman & Todd, 1969.

Hennelly, Alfred T. "The Red-Hot Issue: Liberation Theology," *America*, May 24, 1986, 425-428.

Hunsinger, George. "Karl Barth and Liberation Theology," *Journal of Religion* 1983, 247-263.

Kaiser, Robert B. *Pope, Council and World: The Story of Vatican II*. New York: Macmillan, 1963.

Kearney, Michael, and Bray, Marjorie, eds. "Religion, Resistance, Revolution," *Latin American Perspectives*, Summer 1986, 3-93.

Klaiber, Jeffrey L. *Religion and Revolution in Peru 1824-1976*. Notre Dame: University of Notre Dame Press, 1977.

Kramer, Jane. "Letter from the Elysian Fields," *New Yorker* March 21, 1987, 40-75.

Latourette, Kenneth S. *Christianity in a Revolutionary Age, the Twentieth Century in Europe*. New York: Harper and Brothers, 1961.

Lampe, Armando. "Entre la religiosidad popular y la resistencia popular no hay contradicción," in *Cultura Negra y Teología* (San José, Costa Rica, Conference Papers 1986, 171-176).

Lee, Martin A. "Their Will Be Done," *Mother Jones* July, 1983, 22-27.

Lernoux, Penny. *Cry of the People*. Harmondsworth, England: Penguin, 1982.

Levine, Daniel H. "Religion, the Poor, and Politics in Latin America Today," 3-23, in Daniel H. Levine, ed., *Religion and Political Conflict in Latin America*. Chapel Hill: University of North Carolina Press, 1986.

Libby, Ronald T. "Listen to the Bishops," *Foreign Policy*, Fall 1983, 78-95.

Loveman, Brian. "Military Dictatorship and Political Opposition in Chile, 1973-1986," *Journal of Interamerican Studies,* Winter, 1986/7, 1-38.

Löwy, Michael. *Theologie der Befreiung und Sozialismus* (Frankfurt/Main: Internationale Sozialistische Publikationen, 1987).

MacEoin, Gary. "Latin America Melds Religion, Pragmatism," *NCR* May 22, 1987.

MacEoin, Gary. "Nicaragua: A Church Divided," *America,* November 10, 1984, 294-299.

MacEoin, Gary. "Forming a Catholic Conscience on Social Questions," *Cross Currents,* 1975, 187-197.

Maier, Hans. *Revolution and Church.* Notre Dame: University of Notre Dame Press, 1965.

Mainwaring, Scott. "Brazil: The Catholic Church and the Popular Movement in Nova Iguaçu, 1974-1985" (124-155), in Daniel H. Levine, ed., *Religion and Political Conflict in Latin America.* Chapel Hill: University of North Carolina Press, 1986a.

Mainwaring, Scott. *The Catholic Church and Politics in Brazil 1916-1985.* Stanford: Stanford University Press, 1986b.

Martin, Malachi. *The Jesuits: The Society of Jesus and the Betrayal of the Roman Catholic Church.* New York: Linden Press, 1987.

McCann, Dennis P. "Liberation, the Medellín Conference," *Theology Today,* 1984, 51-60.

McCann, Dennis P. *Christian Realism and Liberation Theology.* Maryknoll, NY: Orbis, 1981.

McGovern, Arthur F. "Liberation Theology in Practice," *Commonweal,* January 28, 1983, 48-49.

McManner, John. *Church and State in France, 1870-1914.* New York: Harper & Row, 1972.

McSweeney, William. *Roman Catholicism.* New York: St. Martin's, 1980.

Mecham, J. Lloyd. *Church and State in Latin America.* Chapel Hill: University of North Carolina Press, 1966.

Messori, Vittorio. *Ratzinger Report.* San Francisco: Ignatius, 1985.

Metz, Johann B. *Die Theologie der Befreiung: Hoffnung oder Gefahr für die Kirche?* Düsseldorf: Patmos, 1986.

Moltmann, Jürgen. *Religion, Revolution, and the Future.* New York: Charles Scribner's Sons, 1969.

Montgomery, Tommie S. "Cross and Rifle: Revolution and the Church in El Salvador and Nicaragua," *Journal of International Affairs,* 1982, 209-221.

Moody, Joseph N. "The Papacy" (21-92), "Catholicism in France" (93-278), "Catholic Development in Spain and Latin America" (721-723), in Joseph N. Moody, ed., *Church and Society: Catholic Social and Political Thought and Movements, 1789-1950.* New York: Arts, 1953.

Neuhaus, Richard J. "A Question of Simple Honesty," *National Review,* May 23, 1986, 37.

Novak, Michael. *The Development of Catholic Thought.* New York: Harper & Row, 1984.

Novak, Michael. "What do they mean by socialism?" *Orbis,* 1986, 405-432.

Novak, Michael. *Will It Liberate? Questions about Liberation Theology.* Mahwah, NJ: Paulist Press, 1987.

O'Brien, Connor C. "God and Man in Nicaragua," *Atlantic Monthly,* August 1986, 50-72.

O'Donohue, John. "Socialist Ideology," in James V. Schall, ed., *Liberation Theology in Latin America.* San Francisco: Ignatius, 1982.

Oviedo, Alvaro, and Mamontov, Stepan. "Theology of Liberation: A New Heresy?" *World Marxist Review,* March 1986, 83-90.

Pablo, Richard. *Death of Christendoms, Birth of the Church: Historical Analysis and Theological Interpretation of the Church in Latin America.* Maryknoll, NY: Orbis, 1987.

Paginas (Lima) "Especial" Documentos #65-66, November/December, 1984.

Peerman, Dan. "CELAM III: Measured Steps Forward," *Christian Century,* April 4, 1979a, 373-378.

Peerman, Dan. "Did the Pope Apply the Brakes at Puebla?" *Christian Century,* February 18, 1979b, 203-204.

Planas, Ricardo. *Liberation Theology: The Political Expression of Religion.* Kansas City, MO: Sheed & Ward, 1986.

Rahner, Karl, et al., eds. *Befreiende Theologie.* Stuttgart: Kohlhammer, 1977.

Rahner, Karl. *Theological Investigations III, VIII.* New York: Herder & Herder, 1971.

Ratté, John. *Three Modernists.* Kansas City, MO: Sheed & Ward, 1967.

Rauscher, Anton. "Lateinamerika braucht die Katholische Soziallehre" (mimeo, n.d.).

Reding, Andrew. "Seeds of a New and Renewed Church: The Ecclesiastical Revolution in Nicaragua," *Monthly Review,* July-August, 1987, 24-55.

Reilly, Charles A. "Latin America's Religious Populists" (42-57), in Daniel H. Levine, ed., *Religion and Political Conflict in Latin America.* Chapel Hill: University of North Carolina Press, 1986.

Riga, Peter J. *The Church and Revolution.* Milwaukee: Bruce, 1967.

Romero, Oscar. *Voices of the Voiceless.* Maryknoll, NY: Orbis, 1985.

Rubenstein, Richard L. "The Political Significance of Latin American Liberation Theology," *International Journal on World Peace,* January–March, 1986, 41-55.

Rubenstein, Richard L., and Roth, John K., eds. *The Politics of Latin American Liberation Theology.* Washington, DC, 1988.

Ruiz, José M. G. "L'Action Française resucitada," *El Pais* (Madrid), June 17, 1988, 15.

Rynne, Xavier. *The Third Session: The Debates and Decrees of Vatican Council II, September 14 to November 21, 1964.* New York: Farrar, Straus & Giroux, 1965.

Scheetz, Thomas. "Liberation Theology is no dry debate in Peru," *NCR,* October 12, 1984.

Shall, James V. *Liberation Theology in Latin America.* San Francisco: Ignatius, 1982.

Seifart, Arnulf. *Der Gott der Politischen Theologie.* Zürich: Benziger, 1987.

Serviço de Intercâmbio Nacional do Movimiento Nacional das Entidades de

Defesea dos Direitos Humanos. *Roma Locuta. Documentos sobre o livro 'Igreja': carisma e poder, Ensaios de eclesiologia militante* de Frei Leonardo Boff. Petrópolis, Brazil: Editora Voces, 1985.

Shiras, Peter. "El Salvador: The New Face of War," *Commonweal,* May 8, 1987, 277-288.

Smith, Brian H. "Chile: Deepening the Allegiance of Working-Class Sectors to the Church in the 1970s" (156-186), in Daniel H. Levine, ed., *Religion and Political Conflict in Latin America.* Chapel Hill: University of North Carolina Press, 1986.

Smith, Brian H. *The Church and Politics in Chile.* Princeton: Princeton University Press, 1982.

Soelle, Dorothee. *Politische Theologie.* Stuttgart: Kreuz, 1982.

Spencer, Philip H. *Politics of Belief.* London: Faber & Faber, 1954.

Sperber, Jonathan. *Popular Catholicism in 19th Century Germany.* Princeton: Princeton University Press, 1984.

Spotts, Frederic. *The Churches and Politics in Germany.* Middletown, CT: Wesleyan University Press, 1973.

Türcke, Christoph. "Halbe Sache," *Merkur,* July 1986, 642-652.

Turner, Frederick C. *Catholicism and Political Development in Latin America.* Chapel Hill: University of North Carolina Press, 1971.

United States Catholic Conference. *Medellín Documents.* Washington, DC: Publication v-170b, "Church in the Present-Day Transformation in Latin America," 1968.

Vidales, Raul. *La Iglesia Latinoamericana y la Politica Después de Medellín.* Bogotá, Colombia: CELAM, 1972.

Vorgrimler, Herbert, ed. *Commentary on the Documents of Vatican II.* New York: Herder & Herder, 1967/8/9, 3 volumes.

Walker, Thomas W. *Nicaragua in Revolution.* New York: Praeger, 1981.

Wallace, Lillian P. *Leo XIII and the Rise of Socialism.* Durham, NC: Duke University Press, 1966.

Welsh, John R. "Communidades Ecclesiais de Base: A New Way to be Church," *America,* February 8, 1986, 85-88.

West, Charles C. *Communism and the Theologians.* Philadelphia: Westminister, 1985.

Whitvliet, Theo. *A Place in the Sun.* Maryknoll, NY: Orbis, 1985.

Whyte, John H. *Catholics in Western Democracies.* New York: St. Martin's, 1981.

Williams, Philip J. "The Catholic Hierarchy in Nicaragua's Revolution," *Journal of Latin American Studies,* November 1985, 341-369.

Zeller, Adrien-Claude. Report of a Trip to Nicaragua. Geneva: Education et Libération, mimeo, May 22, 1983.

Index

About the Author

Werner Levi was born in Halberstadt, Germany. He studied law, sociology, and economics at various universities in Germany, France, and Switzerland. He obtained his doctorate in Jurisprudence and Canon Law at the University of Fribourg, Switzerland. At the University of Minnesota he obtained his Ph.D., in 1944, in Political Science. From 1944 to 1963 he taught at the University of Minnesota. Since then, he has been affiliated with the University of Hawaii at Manoa in the Department of Political Science. Professor Levi has been the recipient of several grants, including two Fulbrights. He has taught and lectured in many foreign countries, among them Germany, Australia, India, Malaysia, Japan, and Denmark. Among his ten books are *The Coming End of War, International Law, International Politics,* and *The Challenge of World Politics in South and Southeast Asia.*

DATE DUE

MAY 22 '91	
APR 13 94	
APR 2 3 1997	

BRODART, INC.   Cat. No. 23-221